Handbook of Positive Prayer

Hypatia Hasbrouck

Unity Books
Unity Village, MO 64065

Fourth Printing 1989

Cover design by Sue Jackson
Cover photo by Tony La Tona

For all the students, counselees, and ministers who asked me to write this book.

Contents

I

About Positive Prayer

And my God will supply every need of yours according to his riches in glory in Christ Jesus. To our God and Father be glory for ever and ever. Amen. (Phil. 4:19, 20)

Positive prayer is not new. It is at least as ancient as Judaism, which nurtured the spiritual life of Jesus from infancy to manhood. It is the form of prayer taught and used by Jesus throughout His ministry, and by His disciples and Paul. It consists of statements such as the above excerpt which acknowledges that God is already supplying whatever good thing we need. A person using positive prayer accepts the gift and gives thanks for it even before it has become apparent. A person using a more traditional kind of prayer may suggest that for some reason God is either withholding what is needed or does not know what is needed. Begging, or imploring, is often used in such a prayer.

Jesus Christ clearly taught the use of positive prayer when in the Sermon on the Mount, He said:

"Therefore I tell you, do not be anxious about your life, what you shall eat or what you shall drink, nor about your body, what you shall put on. Is not life more than food, and the body more than clothing? Look at the birds of the air: they neither sow nor reap nor gather into barns, and yet your heavenly Father feeds them. Are you not of more value than they? And which of you by being anxious can add one cubit to his span of life? And why are you anxious about clothing? Consider the lilies of the field, how they grow; they neither toil nor spin; yet I tell you, even Solomon in all his glory was not arrayed like one of these. But if God so clothes the grass of the field, which today is alive and tomorrow is thrown into the oven, will he not much more clothe you, O men of little faith? Therefore do not be anxious, saying, 'What shall we eat?' or 'What shall we drink?' or 'What shall

we wear?' . . . your heavenly Father knows that you need them all. But seek first his kingdom and his righteousness, and all these things shall be yours as well.

"Therefore do not be anxious about tomorrow, for tomorrow will be anxious for itself. . . . " (Matt. 6:25-34)

Using figures of speech that everyone could understand, Jesus was saying that God is not only the benevolent, generous Father of us all (which He later described in the parable of the prodigal son in Luke 15:11-32), but God is also Divine Mind and the eternal, ever-present, all-wise, all-powerful principle of absolute good, which both governs and acts as the cosmic process that creates and sustains the universe. Jesus knew that God is always at work to supply every created thing with what it requires to express the nature it is created to express. He knew that human beings are created to express the image-likeness of God (Gen. 1:26), and that God, who supplies what birds, lilies, and grass require to express their nature, certainly supplies what humanity requires to express its nature.

Jesus used positive prayer throughout His ministry. He used it when He affirmed the presence of food enough to feed a hungry crowd by first blessing a few loaves and fishes as if they were sufficient; and they were. He used it at the tomb of Lazarus when He said: *"Father, I thank thee that thou hast heard me. I knew that thou hearest me always..."* (John 11:41, 42) and then affirmed the presence of life in Lazarus by commanding him to leave the tomb; and Lazarus did.

Jesus used positive prayer because it was the kind of prayer with which He was most familiar, for positive prayer is the kind most used in Jewish prayer life. If we leaf through The Psalms, we see on almost every page statements that affirm the presence of God and the activity of God in every kind of situation. For instance, Psalms twenty-three is a series of interlocking affirmations which declare that God supplies everything that anyone needs. In His teachings, Jesus directly quoted or referred to The Psalms more than forty times. So steeped in those prayers was He that according to Matthew and Mark, even from the Cross He quoted the first line of Psalms twenty-two—a prayer that affirms the presence of God in the midst of tragedy, and the power of God to transform tragedy into triumph.

His use of positive prayer signified the

total commitment of Jesus to the vision of God as benevolent, generous Father and the eternally active principle of absolute good. If we skim the Gospels, we read passage after passage in which Jesus assures us that God is at work to supply whatever need we recognize. Early in His ministry He said: *"Ask, and it will be given you; seek, and you will find; knock, and it will be opened to you."* (Matt. 7:7) Among His last words during the Crucifixion ordeal were those to the compassionate criminal beside Him: *"Truly, I say to you, today you will be with me in Paradise."* (Luke 23:43)

It is therefore not surprising that according to some scholars the earliest form of the model prayer which Jesus taught His disciples, the Lord's Prayer, was in more positive terms than those in the form we know. According to scholars, Jesus used a tense which would have to be translated this way: Thou art giving us this day our daily bread; Thou art forgiving us our debts, as we are forgiving our debtors, and so on. Perhaps translators considered the phraseology awkward, but whatever the reason for the change, the Lord's Prayer as we know it is a series of simple requests which imply that if we ask, we shall receive. The requests express confidence that God provides the good we seek.

Jesus had utter confidence in God, confidence that was not shaken by the most negative kind of circumstance. Throughout His ministry, He encouraged His followers to develop that same degree of confidence, and during the Last Supper, He summarized His efforts with these words: *". . . the Father who dwells in me does His works." "Truly, truly, I say to you, he who believes in me will also do the works that I do; and greater works than these will he do, because I go to the Father."* (John 14:10, 12)

To believe in Jesus means more than to accept intellectually what He said; it means to *base one's behavior* upon intellectual acceptance of His teaching. Jesus taught His followers to use positive prayer, and He demonstrated the power of positive prayer to accomplish apparent miracles. He wanted them to use positive prayer, for He knew that it would build in them the same confidence that He had in the abiding presence of God that enabled Him to let God work through Him to provide whatever He needed so that He might do whatever He needed to do.

According to the book of The Acts of the

Apostles, the intimate disciples of Jesus who became the apostles practiced positive prayer and were able to do great works. Paul also practiced positive prayer. From his own experience, Paul knew that it transformed one's mind, and so he taught it to everyone who would listen to him or read his letters. He wrote to the Romans: *Do not be conformed to this world but be transformed by the renewal of your mind, that you may prove what is the will of God, what is good and acceptable and perfect.* (Rom. 12:2) To the Ephesians he wrote: *Put off your old nature which belongs to your former manner of life ... and be renewed in the spirit of your minds, and put on the new nature, created after the likeness of God in true righteousness and holiness.* (Eph. 4:22-24)

Paul practiced what he preached; the letters he wrote to the early groups and churches begin with positive prayer statements. If the purpose of the letter was to bolster the faith of the people, Paul thanked God for the faith they had already demonstrated (Rom. 1:8-12); if the purpose was to encourage harmony in the fellowship of believers, he thanked God for the harmonious relationship that already existed. (I Cor.

1:4-9)

Paul's teaching on positive prayer is quite specific. In his first letter to the Thessalonians, he wrote: *Rejoice always, pray constantly, give thanks in all circumstances; for this is the will of God in Christ Jesus for you. Do not quench the Spirit . . . hold fast what is good, abstain from every form of evil.* (I Thess. 5:16-19, 21, 22) Although Paul was advocating that the Thessalonians abstain from evil acts, he was also saying that they should abstain from evil in the form of thoughts of hopelessness, fear, and anxiety— what we today call negative thoughts. Paul knew the power of thought, and in what was probably the last letter he wrote, he advised the Philippians:

Finally, brethren, whatever is true, whatever is honorable, whatever is just, whatever is pure, whatever is lovely, whatever is gracious, if there is any excellence, if there is anything worthy of praise, think about these things. (Phil. 4:8)

If we are to pray constantly, our thoughts must always be consonant with the mind of the Father who dwells within us. By cultivating such thoughts as Paul advocates, we *hold fast what is good* and *do not quench the*

Spirit of God but allow it to do its work through us and for us.

Positive prayer, then, is more than deliberate, conscious communication with God for some specific purpose (although it certainly is that). Positive prayer is the way to form a permanent attitude of mind that reflects the eternal, benevolent activity of God so that we may truly express our nature as the children of God, created in God's image to express God's likeness here on Earth.

II

The How and the Why of Positive Prayer

Many persons may not need to know how and why positive prayer works. To them the information that Jesus taught and used positive prayer is sufficient to warrant their learning and practicing it. This section is included for those who find that knowing how and why a process works helps them to cooperate with it.

The Law of Mind Action

Positive prayer works because of the law of mind action—*thoughts held in mind produce after their kind.* This statement means that if we persistently think a particular kind of thought, other thoughts of the same kind will form in our minds, and eventually we will feel compelled to say the words or do the acts that express the thoughts outwardly so that corresponding conditions or things will be formed in us or in our environment. It also means that we may attract to ourselves or be drawn toward conditions, persons, and things that reflect our persistent thoughts.

The first chapter of Genesis indicates that by a process similar to the law of mind action, God created the universe and all that it contains, including us. First there is an idea in the mind of God, then there is a manifestation that corresponds to the idea. Certainly, that is said about the creation of man: *"Let us make man in our image . . . ." So God created man in his own image, in the image of God He created him . . . .* (Gen. 1:26, 27). An image is the representation of mental vision or an idea. Since we are made to reflect God's idea of Himself, we have the same kind of power that God has, and the ideas or thoughts that we hold in mind are reproducible in the outer or physical world.

Any divine law is simply the way God works, and since God is the principle of absolute good, the law of mind action is intended to bring only good into manifestation. How-

ever, as Jesus pointed out when He said that
God "... *makes his sun rise on the evil and on
the good, and sends rain on the just and on
the unjust*" (Matt. 5:45), God's absolute
goodness is impersonal; thus, the law of mind
action operates impersonally. Rather like a
perfectly constructed computer which gives
right solutions to problems only if we feed it
with right information, the law of mind action can give us what is right and good for us
only if we feed it with right and good
thoughts. In the words of computer opera-
tors, "Good stuff in, good stuff out. Garbage
in, garbage out."

Charles Fillmore, cofounder of Unity
School of Christianity, pointed out in many of
his writings that divine law produces results
for us according to how we exercise our own
willpower. Because we are made to express
the image-likeness of God, and God has abso-
lutely free will, we have free will. We can
choose our habitual thoughts. If we wish to
have good in our lives, we need to choose
thoughts that produce only good. Myrtle Fillmore, wife of Charles Fillmore and cofounder
of Unity, wrote: *Never make an assertion, no
matter how true it may look on the surface,
that you do not want continued or repro-*

duced . . . . In the practice of positive prayer, we deliberately choose thoughts which focus on the good we desire rather than on the loss, lack, or limitation we may be experiencing. In prayer, we learn to avoid thinking or speaking about unwanted conditions and to concentrate upon the perfect outcome of challenges.

Oneness

The law of mind action operates in three modes. The first mode is oneness. God-Mind is one with its ideas even after the ideas manifest in the material world, for the very stuff which underlies everything in the material world is the substance of God. It is true that God is infinite and transcendent; in simple words, this means that God has no boundaries, that there are aspects of God above and beyond our comprehension, and that there is more God than there are God-ideas and God-substance. But God is also immanent, ever present as the underlying substance of material things, the innate intelligence within them, and the principle which gives them life or activity. In other words, God is one with creation. God is omnipresent. The writer of

Psalms 139 testified to Judaism's recognition of the immanence or omnipresence of God when he wrote:

Whither shall I go from thy Spirit?
Or whither shall I flee from thy presence?
If I ascend to heaven, thou art there!
If I make my bed in Sheol, thou art there!
If I take the wings of the morning and
dwell in the uttermost parts of the sea,
even there thy hand shall lead me,
and thy right hand shall hold me.

(Psalms 139:7-10)

Those lines, incidentally, ought to be among the memorized prayers of anyone who wishes to practice positive prayer; for, saying or thinking them often reminds one that God is always available.

Because we are created to express the image of God, we are one with our habitual thoughts and one with the activity of the law of mind action. We cannot escape the results of our own thinking; just as the ideas in God-Mind become manifest in the material realm, so our habitual thoughts, unless we deliberately work to dissolve the undesirable ones, will manifest in some way at some time in our bodies or circumstances. The method used to dissolve undesirable thoughts is called *denial;* it will be discussed in the section on Denial and Affirmation.

Charles Fillmore stressed our responsibility for the circumstances of our lives. He wrote:

Remember that man makes all appearance and names it good or evil according to the pleasure it gives him. God furnishes the raw material, as it were, out of which this appearance is formed, and this is always good, because its pure essence cannot be polluted.

If man combines the life, love, substance, and intelligence of Principle in such a way that discord results, let him not lay it to God. Man is a free agent, and in the exercise of his freedom he has left out some factor in forming his world. What that factor is he can only discover by asking God direct; and he must not omit to ask with all the fervor of his nature.

We can discover how to combine *the life, love, substance, and intelligence of Principle in such a way* that harmony rather than discord results because the mind of each of us is a focal point in God-Mind.

Since the mind of each of us is one with

God-Mind, the minds of all of us must also be connected. The majority of metaphysicians believe that our minds are connected in what they call *race mind.* Race mind is thought to contain everything that humankind has ever experienced and to receive every thought that anyone thinks right now. Certainly there seems to be evidence that race mind exists: frequently the same new concepts seem to be expressed in widely separated areas at much the same time; mental communication seems to be possible between persons who have a close relationship. For this reason, the mode of oneness makes our own mental health important both to ourselves and to the entire human race.

The mode of oneness is also called the principle of oneness and the force that we know as love.

Order

The second mode in which the law of mind action works is called *order.* Order establishes the right sequence for events. The first chapter of Genesis tells us that God creates by a sequential or orderly process. Some divine ideas must become manifest before other divine ideas can become manifest. According to Genesis, God performed many creative acts before saying: *"Let us make man in our image...."* The divine ideas which make an environment suitable for the manifestation of God's image come into being first.

So, order is often called *right timing.* As the ancient preacher observed: *For everything there is a season, and a time for every matter under heaven.* (Eccles. 3:1) And Jesus said: *"... first the blade, then the ear, then the full grain in the ear."* (Mark 4:28)

Order also governs right relationships among things. Everything has its right place, and when by some means it is in wrong relationship to the things about it, order makes an adjustment to reestablish the right relationship. Adjustment is called *justice* when it is active in some kinds of human affairs.

Circulation

The third mode is *circulation.* Divine ideas and divine substance eternally circulate from God or the unmanifest realm, into the manifest realm, and back to the unmanifest. In the manifest or material realm, circulation governs life processes such as breathing and blood flow: if circulation stops, an organism stops. It governs material environment: if the free circulation of air stops, the atmosphere becomes stale; if the circulation of water stops, the lake becomes stagnant. Circulation governs the economy: if the circulation of goods and money stops, the economy stops. There is no way to escape circulation.

After realizing that circulation governs us, the most important point to remember is that circulation always brings us more of whatever we circulate. God sends into manifestation one idea of His own image, but countless individualized replicas of that idea become manifest and eventually return to God. In like manner, what we send forth returns to us in kind and multiplied. Certainly our thoughts do, as the story of Job illustrates when, after his many afflictions, Job cries out: "... *the thing that I fear comes upon me* ...." (Job 3:25)

The law of mind action is intended to produce only good, and it will when we learn how to cooperate with it in all three modes. We can learn by practicing positive prayer.

Attention

To practice positive prayer we must focus our attention upon Truth rather than facts. To practitioners of positive prayer, the word *Truth* refers to the invisible, eternal realm of God-Mind and the spiritual principles which govern creation. The basic Truth may be stated this way: *There is only one Presence and one power active in the universe, God, the good.* If we accept this Truth, we cannot accept belief in any invisible, eternal, spiritual presence, power, activity, or principle opposed to God; for there can be no idea in God-Mind to account for it.

The word *fact* refers to circumstances, conditions, and things which appear in the visible, temporal, material world. Facts are experienced through the senses in some way. They are the way the material world seems to be, and they are subject to change and interpretation. That is the state of even scientific facts, for they, too, deal with the material world.

Truth, then, is enduring. It is of God, and God is enduring; so Truth is ultimately real. Facts are changeable; they only seem real. Truth is powerful because it is of God. Facts have only the power that we ascribe to them at any moment, for we make the facts with our own perception and thought about the material world. Facts are appearances.

The more attention we pay to something, the more important and influential it becomes in our lives. That is why positive prayer focuses attention upon Truth or only those facts which are accurate reflections of Truth.

Denial and Affirmation

Much praying is stimulated by negative facts (those which do not accurately reflect Truth) or appearances which we mistakenly believe have power to take or keep some good from us. When faced with negative appearances, the practitioner of positive prayer withdraws attention from the appearance by making a *denial.* He speaks, silently or aloud, words which declare the unreality and powerlessness of the appearance. Then he focuses attention upon Truth by immediately making an affirmation. He does this by speaking, silently or aloud, words which declare the presence of God and good.

For instance, suppose a man who practices

positive prayer loses his job. At first, like most anyone, he might react with fear, anger, and worry; but, quickly he will be likely to remember a more constructive way to deal with the apparently adverse situation. It is to deny power to the situation with words such as these: The lack of a job is powerless to take or keep my good from me. Then he would affirm the presence of good with words such as these: *There is a perfect job at perfect pay where I can serve in a perfect way awaiting me right now. Thank You, Father.* Any thoughts of fear or worry over finding a job can then become reminders to repeat the affirmation, and soon he will be focusing his attention upon the solution rather than the problem. The solution is the perfect job at perfect pay where he can serve in a perfect way, so when he looks at ads for employment or hears about open jobs, he will be alert to a perfect job.

Notice that a denial is used once, but an affirmation is repeated many times. Because a denial acknowledges the existence of a negative appearance, frequent repetition of a denial focuses attention upon the negative appearance and increases rather than decreases belief in its power; but an affirmation focuses attention upon Truth—that God provides whatever we need—and frequent repetition increases belief in the power of God to lead us to the good we seek or to draw that good to us.

Notice, too, that a denial does not declare that the negative appearance does not exist; it declares that the negative appearance is powerless over us. It is, by the way, important to formulate denials as positively as possible because, as psychologists have discovered, the subconscious mind tends to respond best to key words or long words in sentences. Why this is so, we do not know; but we do know that teachers have discovered that pupils frequently overlook words like *no* and *not* when they read and often do not seem to hear them when they are spoken.

The Three Phases of Mind

Prayer is a mental act; and so, to understand how and why positive prayer works, we need to have some understanding of the three phases of mind and their interaction.

We are most familiar with the conscious phase of mind; indeed, this is the phase of mind which is most personal. With the conscious phase of mind we actively notice the outer world, think, reason, make decisions, form beliefs, and judge ourselves, other persons, and our world. Though the conscious mind connects us with the material world and does many things, it is the smallest phase of mind, for it operates only in the present moment and only when a person is awake and aware.

The subconscious phase of mind is much greater, and it always operates, for it contains the blueprint and operating instructions for the human body. We do not consciously keep our hearts beating, blood circulating, or lungs breathing; nor do we consciously mend cuts on the skin or knit broken bones. These are functions of the subconscious phase of mind which also runs all the biochemical processes of the body.

In addition, the subconscious phase of mind is the memory bank; it records all the voluntary muscle actions that we learn so that once we have learned to walk, ride a bicycle, type, or play the piano, the subconscious mind does most of the work, and we do not have to think about each part of the action. As the memory bank, the subconscious mind also records all impressions of which we are not fully conscious, plus every thought we think, every word we speak, and every action we perform. The moment we think a thought or say a word, the thought or word goes into the memory bank. The more often we think the thought or say the word, the more firmly it is set in the memory bank.

In addition to all the foregoing work, the subconscious mind is in charge of our feelings and emotions. When strong feelings are connected with memories, the memories are particularly powerful and can influence the way the conscious phase of mind responds to events in the present that resemble the powerful memories.

The subconscious mind also contains the intuitive faculty, which is the direct connection with other human minds (race mind) and the superconscious phase of mind (the Mind of God in us).

The superconscious phase of mind is the source of inspiration; it is the still small voice of God which speaks in the silence after prayer, offering comfort and guidance. However, since the superconscious mind is reached through the subconscious mind, it is important to clear obstructions from the subconscious mind.

Obstructions are the erroneous, negative, or no longer appropriate thoughts, beliefs, and attitudes that have accumulated in our personal memory banks and which limit our ability to receive and accept messages from God. The principle work of denials is to clear away those obstructions. The principal work of affirmations is to form a mental environment which can receive and accept messages from God, an environment formed of thoughts, feelings, beliefs, and attitudes in harmony with God-Mind.

III

To Pray Constantly

Paul advised the Thessalonians to pray constantly. Since prayer connects us consciously with God-Mind, we would be wise to follow Paul's advice. The practice of positive prayer helps us develop mental habits which constitute a state very like constant prayer— one in which we, like Brother Lawrence, *practice the presence of God.*

A noted advocate of positive prayer, H. Emilie Cady, said: *Practice the presence of God just as you would practice music.* The analogy is apt. Persons who wish to master the piano must practice on it every day for specific periods of time. They must do five-finger exercises over and over until their fingers respond perfectly to what their eyes see on the page or their mental ears hear.

They must practice until they do not even think about individual notes but are completely one with the music they play. Even after they become accomplished pianists, they must return often to five-finger exercises and practice daily. Significantly, as their sense of oneness with music grows, so does the length of their practice times.

To master positive prayer, we need to be as regular and disciplined in prayer as musicians are in music. When we are regular and disciplined in prayer, we are more willing to keep our thoughts positive because we realize that, since we are in the presence of God at all times and in all places, every thought can be a prayer.

It is far easier to establish conscious prayer habits than most of us think. Actually, anyone who reads a book such as this is probably already engaged in some fairly regular prayer activity. The following daily prayer pattern has helped many persons establish prayer habits that lead to the practice of the presence of God. You will probably discover that you need add only a few steps.

Daily Prayer Pattern

1. *Begin each day with private prayer and meditation.*

Many persons use a daily devotional booklet for their morning prayer time. Individuals who have an exercise period often begin and end it with brief meditations and say or think short prayers during rest periods. During the morning prayer period, it is particularly wise to impress upon the mind the three modes in which the law of mind action operates—oneness, order, and circulation. Here are appropriate affirmations:

Oneness: *My mind is one with the Mind of God.*

Order: *With Godlike thoughts, I think a Godlike world into being.*

Circulation: *I send forth only thoughts of good, and good returns in overflowing measure.*

(Say each one three times to impress it upon the conscious, subconscious, and superconscious phases of mind.)

It does not matter how long the morning prayer time is; it can be from five minutes to an hour. Most persons find that a period of twenty to thirty minutes starts their day with the right thoughts to prepare them to recognize all the good that surrounds them and to be ready to deal positively with whatever challenges the day brings.

2. *Bless every meal.*

This step reminds us three times a day (oftener if we have snacks) that God is the source of our good. It also tends to relax us so that we can enjoy and benefit from our food. If you are in public and do not wish to be conspicuous, a silent "Thank You, Father" or similar thought will suffice. However, families have been observed saying table blessings aloud in restaurants all over the world, and no one has objected. Some airlines have table blessings of various faiths printed on their menus. Apparently, people are beginning to recognize the importance of blessing food.

3. *Use the phrase "I am" to preface only positive statements.*

This practice can make a dramatic change in you and in your life. The phrase "I am" says, in effect, that we identify ourselves with whatever feeling, thought, characteristic, or condition follows; therefore, we need to be careful to follow "I am" with only the feelings, thoughts, characteristics, and conditions with which we want to be identified and which we want to have continued or reproduced in our characters and experiences.

This step is not particularly easy because we use many expressions which, taken literally, have negative meanings. Many people habitually apologize with the words, "I'm sorry," or preface unwelcome information with the words, "I'm afraid that." If you would rather not chance feeling sorry or afraid, you can use one of several methods to break the habit of using expressions with negative connotations. You may want to ask someone with whom you spend a lot of time to call your attention to every such expression so that you can immediately substitute a positive one. You may want to simply listen to yourself and interrupt every negative expression by changing the words. You may want to immediately think "Erase" or "Cancel" and then change the words. You may find it helpful to visualize the negative expression and then imagine that you are drawing a large black X across it. Many people carry a small pocket notebook in which to write any unwanted expressions they may inadvertently use; they then draw an X or a heavy line through the words and as soon as possible tear up the page and throw it away or burn it. Use any method that is effective for you.

Remember that it is important to find positive ways to say exactly what you mean. For instance, replace "I'm sorry" with "I apologize." That is, after all, what you mean. Change "I'm afraid you have the wrong number" to "You have the wrong number." As you find ways to speak more accurately, you stop feeding your subconscious mind with misinformation about yourself. You also cease taking the name of the Lord in vain.

Perhaps the last remark surprises you. According to the Bible, I AM is the only name of God that was directly revealed to anyone. Moses received the revelation along with the commission to free the Israelites from Egyptian bondage. When Moses asked what he should say to the people, God said: *"Say this to the people of Israel, 'I AM has sent me to you.' "* (Exod. 3:14) So, I AM is the name of God, and every time we use these words we are, in a sense, praying, for we are claiming kinship with God.

4. *Speak and act as if you already are as you wish to become.*

As Paul observed, in God we live and move

and have our being. Whether we realize it or not, all our words and acts are connected with the creative source and are, therefore, creative. They form our characters and our part in every experience we have. If, for instance, we wish to have positive relationships with all persons in our lives, we need to speak and act as if we already have such relationships— to speak positively to and about even the most apparently difficult individuals; to treat them with the consideration with which we want them to treat us; to praise them for the good they do; and, above all, to silently affirm that they are wise and kind.

5. *Dedicate every word and act to the glory of God.*

Since we live and move and have our being in God, whatever we are saying or doing, we are saying and doing in the presence of God, and every word, or act, is a kind of prayer. If we consciously dedicate every word and act to the glory of God, we may find that there are some words and acts that we cannot so dedicate. We know then that we need to eliminate them.

Be patient with yourself. Forgive yourself and thank God for bringing each error to your awareness, and use suggestions given in this book to help you eliminate the words and acts from your life.

6. *Fill idle-thought time with affirmations, memorized prayers, and brief meditations.*

This step effectively prevents thoughts about unpleasant matters from taking over our minds. As we practice this step, we will notice that it can reduce the number of annoying situations with which we must deal. For instance, suppose someone keeps you waiting beyond the appointed time; rather than thinking about the inconvenience, or worrying about what might have happened to the other person, or becoming angry, think prayer thoughts. When the person arrives, you will be calm and pleasant, or if (as rarely happens) there really is an emergency, you will be in a mental condition which allows you to deal with it. Even while you are forming the habit of filling idle-thought time with prayer thoughts, you will begin to welcome such moments and be grateful for them.

7. *Ignore the speck in your brother's or sister's eye.*

Jesus said quite clearly that our main business is to reform ourselves, not other persons. (Matt. 7:3-5) If, throughout the day, we must deal with individuals who make negative remarks or behave unkindly or irresponsibly, we need to monitor our thoughts, words, and acts to be sure that we are not allowing other persons to determine how we think, speak, and behave. The positive prayer response to the apparently negative words and acts of others is the silent use of denials and affirmations. For instance, if someone loses his temper, silently deny with these words that his temper has the power to disturb you: (John's) temper is powerless to take or keep my good from me. Then silently affirm: *I am poised and centered, and you are poised and centered, in the peace of God.* You will find that you will not react to the display of temper and you will be able to remain calm.

8. *End each day with private prayer.*

We can use any prayers we wish to close the day, but the last prayers should always include thanksgiving for all the good the day has brought and for all the opportunities to learn and grow that we have experienced. It is well, also, to use again the three affirmations for oneness, order, and circulation suggested earlier to fix them firmly in the subconscious memory bank. In addition, we need to place concern about the welfare of others into God's care. A good way to conclude a

day of prayer is to affirm that you and everyone for whom you pray are surrounded by
God's light and love and protected by His
presence.

As you practice the daily prayer pattern,
the quality of your life will improve, for your
mind will become aligned with the creative
activity of God-Mind. You will be cooperat-
ing with the law of mind action in all three
modes, and you will be habitually thinking
the kinds of thoughts you wish to have manifest in your life. You will become progressive-
ly more open to receive and act upon divine
ideas that come to you so that more good
manifests in your body and circumstances.

In the Name and Through the
Power of Jesus Christ

Jesus directed His followers to pray in His
name. The improvements in your life will ac-
celerate and escalate if you will close every
prayer with the familiar words, "In the name
and through the power of Jesus Christ."
Each time you say or think these words, you
impress upon your mind the truth about
yourself as a son or daughter of God with the
potential for expressing that spiritual reality

just as did Jesus Christ. In Christian thought, at least, Jesus best exemplifies what it means to be the spiritual offspring of God, born to serve as a channel for God's activity for good in this world.

The familiar words, "In the name and through the power of Jesus Christ," are more than a conventional expression. Properly understood, they constitute a mighty affirmation. The word *name* is more than a collection of sounds which designates a thing or a person; it also means *character*. So, when we declare that we are praying "in the name" of Jesus Christ, we affirm that while we pray we have the same kind of consciousness or character He had—one marked by absolute faith in God and willingness to carry out God's will for the good of all humankind.

In addition, to do anything "in the name" of a leader means to do it "by the authority" of that leader. So, when we go directly to God in prayer and do it "in the name" of Jesus Christ, we do it by His authority. We are obeying His instructions.

If we add "and through the power of Jesus Christ," we declare that the creative activity of God works as surely through us as it worked through Jesus.

We can see why the understanding use of this familiar expression can work wonders in us and in our lives.

The same is true for the use of the word *Amen.*

A Word About Amen

Amen may be used as often as we wish when we pray. Ordinarily, it is said only at the close of prayer; but there is no reason that we should not say it after every affirmation. *Amen* is a Hebrew word that means *so it is; so shall it be; so be it.* It also means *certainly* or *truly,* and *this is true.* When we know what the word means, we can see why we can use it freely as long as we use it after a positive statement or prayer. Obviously, we would not want to add amen to words like these, "Father, help me. I have no money and I am hungry." These may be the facts of a present situation, but we would not want to say "so it is; so shall it be; so be it" to the continuation of poverty and hunger. We need to be careful to say amen to Truth and Truth only.

For centuries, devout individuals of many faiths have tacked amen onto the ends of all kinds of prayers. Could it be that in doing so they have ratified negative statements and helped to continue unwanted conditions? We cannot know the answer; but we can certainly avoid ratifying the negative for ourselves.

By ratifying only what is true, only what reflects God's ongoing creative activity, we constantly adjust our thinking to that activity and form new habits of thought. This is a way we become *transformed by the renewal of our minds.*

Yes, regular, disciplined prayer changes you. It does not change the way God treats you. There is no need to change the way God treats any of us, for God's activity is always for the highest good of all parts of creation, including us. Prayer changes us so that we no longer unwittingly block the activity of God; instead, we cooperate with it.

Our prayers do not change other persons. Other persons may seem to change when, through prayer, we change our perception and understanding of them. They may actually change in response to the new way we treat them as a result of our new perception and understanding of them, but the change we may see will result from the change in their perception of us.

Speaking of other persons, unless we have

begun to practice positive prayer in partnership with another person, it is best not to share with anyone our experience with prayer. Persons not involved in positive prayer rarely understand the inner process. They may express boredom, skepticism, or cynicism. Such attitudes can dampen our enthusiasm at a crucial point and place needless obstacles in our way. In addition, even though our motive in sharing may be to encourage loved ones to engage in the practice of positive prayer so that they can reap the same benefits we enjoy, our sharing can have the opposite effect. If they are not ready to undertake the discipline, they may misconstrue our enthusiasm as an effort to force our way upon them.

The best way to encourage others to practice positive prayer is to persist in our own prayer life. The good results will speak more convincingly for us than our words. As our lives become more orderly, our circumstances more prosperous, our bodies more healthy, our behavior more kindly, our work more productive, and our attitudes more joyful, the people in our lives will want to know how we have achieved such changes. Then is the time to share.

Prayer Partners

Perhaps you are beginning the practice of positive prayer with one or more partners. If so, your experiences can be rich, indeed, for Jesus said: "... *where two or three are gathered in my name, there am I in the midst of them.*" (Matt. 18:20) Although most of the daily prayer pattern is to guide you in private communion with God, parts of it can be shared with family members, should they be your prayer partners. Even if you are in partnership, each partner must have private communion with God. But prayer partners can share specific prayer times and prayer activities in addition to those in the daily prayer pattern. The following suggestions have enhanced the experiences of many persons in prayer partnership:

1. *Set a definite time to meet regularly.*

Keep the appointment as you would an appointment with a counselor or physician or for a tennis, golf, or bridge lesson. Meet at least once a week or more often, and reserve at least fifteen minutes for prayer—more if you wish. If you wish to socialize too, separate the prayer and the social activities.

2. *Decide whether or not you will use a spe-*

cific format and what it will be.

You may decide always to pray a particular prayer such as the Lord's Prayer or the Twenty-Third Psalm at the beginning of your time together. You may wish to use a devotional booklet, affirmations, spontaneous prayers, or all of them. How you spend your prayer time is your choice.

3. *Pray about one another's concerns.*

You may use affirmations from this book, or design them to fit your specific needs. The concerns may be personal or may involve other persons. The important thing is that you are praying about them together and that your joint prayers strengthen your ability to let God do His perfect work in and through you both.

4. *Set a specific time when you will not be together but will pray the same prayer.*

Again, this may be only once a week, but most partners prefer to have more frequent prayer times. To know that someone is praying the same prayer at the same time gives you a great sense of your oneness in Spirit.

5. *Feel free to call one another for prayer support.*

Often (when we are deeply involved in a situation) we feel that we need to let someone else do the praying. Let your prayer partner pray for you until you feel you can pray in faith.

6. *Keep confidentiality.*

Prayer partners share their concerns with one another. Never divulge shared information without the consent of the person. If you are concerned about your partner, take the concern to God in prayer, and see your partner enjoying the perfect outcome.

7. *Be flexible and ready to dissolve the partnership when it has done its work.*

It may be necessary to rearrange meeting times. Either of you may wish to change the regular prayers you use. Be willing to do whatever is needed to keep the partnership a satisfactory experience. If you feel that the partnership has served its purpose, be willing to dissolve it. Most partnerships never completely end. The partners may no longer meet, but the bond between them is spiritual, and so it continues. Many partners feel free to call or write one another for prayer support even years after they have ceased to meet regularly.

A Prayer Journal

Prayer partners can share the experiences they have as a result of prayer. But whether or not you have a prayer partner, you will find keeping a private prayer journal a valuable practice. The journal need not be elaborate; a composition book or a loose-leaf binder will do. In the journal, record what you have learned as a result of your prayer work, what experiences you have had, the evidence of answered prayer that you have received. You may wish to record specific insights or ideas. You may make entries daily or weekly, as you choose. You will find that keeping a prayer journal helps you to persist in prayer, because when you review what you have written, you can see how your improving inner life has changed your material life for the better.

IV

The Use of Denial and Affirmation

A daily prayer pattern calls for the use of denials and affirmations. Although there are many classic denials that have helped individuals change from a negative to a positive way of thinking about and responding to life, there is one denial that can be easily adapted to help you quickly deal positively with almost any negative appearance or challenge the moment it arises.

The All-Purpose Denial

I call it *the all-purpose denial.* Two adaptations have already been offered in this book. Here is the basic form: (This) is powerless to take or keep my good from me. In place of the word *this,* you can substitute a phrase describing the negative appearance or challenge.

Denial is a necessary step to take for the sake of the subconscious mind. In the past, we have customarily accepted negative appearances as powerful realities which determine our lives. Now that we are practicing positive prayer, we are recognizing that negative appearances are not ultimately real and have only the power we are willing to give them. The denial states our unwillingness to give power to anything that threatens to take or keep our good in any form from us. When we think or say denials, we tell our subconscious minds that they are not to react to the negative appearances but are to act upon the affirmations, which we then make. The process opens us to receive whatever divine idea we need to deal positively with the appearance and prepares us to allow the activity of God to do its perfect work.

To impress the all-purpose denial upon your subconscious mind so that you remember it when you need it, you might wish to write an appropriate adaptation to precede each suggested affirmation in the following list of affirmations. A space has been provided, and a few sample adaptations have been inserted. To impress both the denial and the affirmation upon the subconscious mind, after you have written your adaptation of the all-purpose denial, if the affirmation has any relevance to your present life, say both the denial and the affirmation aloud.

Suggested Affirmations

The daily prayer pattern advocates the use of affirmations to help you respond positively to specific situations. Some affirmations in the following list have words in parentheses to show how to adapt them for others or for application to specific situations. You might wish to copy the affirmations that most appeal to you in a small notebook to carry with you. Then you can find an appropriate affirmation when a situation arises. Some of the most frequent prayer needs have been listed. The order is alphabetical to make it easy for you to copy them in a convenient sequence. You might also wish to include in your notebook your adaptation of the all-purpose denial before each affirmation you choose.

Prayer Need	*Affirmation*
Employment	Denial—The lack of a job is powerless to take or keep my (your) good from me (you). *There is the perfect job at the perfect pay open for me (you) right now.*
Forgiveness	Denial—This offense (insult, snub, unkindness, etc.) is powerless to take or keep my good from me. *The freeing love of God liberates me (you) from mistakes of the past and the results of the mistakes of the past. I am (You are) a new creation through the power of God (or the Christ) within me (you).*
General	Denial—This situation is powerless to take or keep my (your) good from me (you).

Prayer Need	*Affirmation*

What God has done for others, He can do for me (you), and more.

Guidance   Denial— _____

_____

1. *The light of God illumines my way.*
2. *God reveals right answers in this situation.*
3. *With God, I know what to do, and I do it.*

Harmony   Denial— _____

_____

Divine love establishes understanding, joy, and peace in my heart (your heart, this situation, the hearts of all concerned).

Healing   Denial— _____

_____

Prayer Need	*Affirmation*

God's healing life flows through me now, restoring me (my arm, my feet, my eyes, etc.) to wholeness and perfection.

Joy

Denial— _____
_____

1. *The joy of God fills my heart and mind right now.*
2. *As a child of God, happiness is my heritage.*

Judgment

Denial— _____
_____

1. *God gives me good judgment. I know what to do and I do it.*
2. *I judge righteously in the light of Truth.*

Justice

Denial— _____
_____

1. *Divine justice is at work in this situation.*

Prayer Need	*Affirmation*
	2. *What is mine by divine right is mine right now.*

Lost Persons, Animals, or Things	Denial—(This is a specific denial for this prayer need.) No one (nothing) is lost in Spirit.

1. *God is revealing the whereabouts of _____ to me (to the searchers).*
2. *God is guiding me (you, the searchers) to _____ .*
3. *God is protecting _____ until I (you, they) find _____ .*

Love	Denial— _____ _____

1. *I am God's beloved, lovable, loving child.*
2. *Through God's love in my heart, I am one with you, and you are one with me.*

Prayer Need	*Affirmation*

Memory

Denial— _____

_____

1. *I know, I understand, and I express myself perfectly.*
2. *God gives me a perfect memory.*

Order

Denial— _____

_____

1. *Divine order is established in me and in this situation.*
2. *Divine love establishes divine order in all that concerns me.*

Peace of Mind

Denial— _____

_____

1. *Divine love now dissolves and dissipates all anxious, confused, or fearful thoughts, and I am peaceful in mind and heart.*
2. *I am poised and centered in the peace of God (Christ).*

Prayer Need	*Affirmation*
Power	Denial—Other persons (outer circumstances) are powerless to take or keep my good from me.
	God gives me the right words to speak (the right things to do) in the right way at the right time.
Prosperity	Denial— _____
	1. *God supplies all that I need when I need it, and I am open and receptive to my good.*
	2. *As I freely share my good, I am open to accept the good that supplies my need.*
Protection	Denial— _____
	1. *The Lord goes before me, making easy and safe my way.*

Prayer Need	*Affirmation*

2. *There is but one Presence and one Power, God, the good.*
3. *Wherever I am, God is with me.*
4. *I am safe in the everlasting arms of God.*

Release   Denial— _____

                         _____

1. *I now release you (this situation, this belief); I loose you (it); I let you (it) go; and I let God have His perfect way with you (it).*
2. *I let go and I let God.*
3. *I place you (this situation) lovingly in God's hands.*

Spiritual
Growth   Denial—My apparent human flaws are powerless to prevent my spiritual growth.

Prayer Need	*Affirmation*
	Moment by moment, step by step, my indwelling Lord transforms me into a living, loving expression of the image and likeness of God, my heavenly Father.
Strength	Denial— _____ _____
	1. *I can do all things through the Spirit of God (Christ) which strengthens me.*
	2. *Through the strength of God (Christ), I persevere and do what I must do.*
Success	Denial— _____ _____
	As God's child, I am born to succeed.
Transition (Death)	Denial—The cessation of earthly life is powerless to sever the bonds of love, for life and love are eternal.

Prayer Need   *Affirmation*

    1. *He (She) is moving into
       the eternal light of God.*
    2. *The peace of God fills my
       mind and heart as I re-
       lease* _____
       into God's loving hands.

Understanding Denial— _____

_____

*I understand that God is the
light, life, and love within me
and the law that works to
bring good into my life.*

Will   Denial— _____

_____

    1. *God's perfect will for good
       is done in and through me
       now.*
    2. *God reveals His will to
       me, and I do it.*

Composing Affirmations

Although these affirmations have been carefully constructed, there is nothing sacred or magical about the words that are used. If any words are awkward for you, feel free to change them. As you become accustomed to using affirmations, you will probably begin to compose your own to deal with specific situations. You can begin right now to transform conventional prayer statements into affirmations. The method is simple.

1. Begin any prayer statement with either "I know that" or "I give thanks that (or for)."
2. Use the present tense forms throughout the prayer, and whenever possible insert the word *now*.

The words, "I know that" or "I give thanks that (or for)" are rather like the training wheels on a child's first bicycle. They keep us steady. So, if you have a health challenge, instead of beseeching God by saying, "God, please heal me," say, "I know that God is healing me now" and "I give thanks that God is healing me now."

Many great prayers are written in the affirmative mode; others can easily be changed into it. The following lines from the Prayer of St. Patrick can be prayed by any practitioner of positive prayer. In fact, this prayer would be a good choice for inclusion in your morning or night prayer time.

Prayer of St. Patrick

* * *

I take for my sureties:
The power of God to guide me,
The might of God to uphold me,
The wisdom of God to teach me,
The eye of God to watch over me,
The ear of God to hear me,
The word of God to give me speech,
The hand of God to protect me,
The way of God to go before me,
The shield of God to shelter me, . . .
Christ (is) with me, Christ before me,
Christ behind me, Christ within me,
Christ beneath me, Christ above me,
Christ at my right, Christ at my left . . .
Christ in the heart of every man who
    thinks of me,

> Christ in the mouth of every man who
>   speaks to me,
> Christ in every eye that sees me,
> Christ in every ear that hears me—

Only the word *is,* in parentheses in the tenth line, is a substitution for the word in the usual translation of the prayer. It was originally *be,* but because the imperative tense suggests that the Christ might not be present, it was changed to the present tense. The Christ is the perfect spiritual image-likeness of God which is the true, if unexpressed, spiritual self of every person; so the Christ is always present in all of us, whether or not we know it or are expressing it. If, for any reason, you feel uncomfortable about using the word Christ in connection with yourself, you can still pray the prayer and substitute the words "the image of God" for it.

Regardless of the word or words you use, if you elect to pray this prayer frequently, you will stimulate your spiritual growth because you will impress the truth about yourself upon both the conscious and subconscious phases of your mind.

Prayer of St. Francis

Another great prayer that stimulates spiritual growth and can easily be changed into the affirmative mode is the popular and beloved Prayer of St. Francis. In the usual translation, the first two lines are: *Lord, make me an instrument of Your peace. Where there is hatred let me sow love* .... The words that are in regular type have been changed to make the prayer affirmative:

Lord, I am *an instrument of Your peace.*
Where there is hatred I *sow love;*
where there is injury, pardon;
where there is doubt, faith;
where there is despair, hope;
where there is darkness, light;
and where there is sadness, joy.

In the second part of the prayer, only a few small changes make the entire prayer one for the realization of spiritual growth in this present lifetime. The original first clause of the second part is: *O divine Master, grant that I may not so much seek to be consoled as to console* .... The final clause is: ... *it is in dying that we are born to eternal life.* Notice the effect of the small changes:

> *O divine Master,* I do *not so much seek*
> *to be consoled as to console;*
> *to be understood as to understand;*
> *to be loved as to love.*
> *For it is in giving that we receive;*
> *it is in pardoning that we are pardoned;*
> *and it is in dying* to the human self
> *that we are born* into the *eternal* Christ.

The more frequently you pray either of these prayers, the more firmly the truth is impressed upon your consciousness. You may find appropriate lines coming to mind to serve as affirmations in moments of need. For instance, if you observe that someone is angry or combative, the line, *"Lord,* I am *an instrument of Your peace,"* may sound within you to remind you to respond in a way that will not increase the anger or combativeness. Or if you are in a situation which arouses fear in you, you may remember the words, "The hand of God to protect me" or "The shield of God to shelter me." Such brief statements can calm you so that you can deal in the best possible way with the situation.

That is the very practical function of the

daily prayer pattern and affirmations—to help us deal with the challenges of our earthly lives in ways appropriate for the beloved children of God so that we enjoy the benefits of being God's offspring.

V

The Seven-Step Prayer

In your morning and nighttime prayers, you are free to choose any prayers you wish. If you feel the need to establish order among the prayers, you may want to design a seven-step prayer for your use. The seven steps are as follows:

1. Illumination: You affirm the presence of God.
2. Adoration: You offer praise and thanksgiving for God's presence in your life.
3. Forgiveness: You accept God's forgiveness of your errors, and you forgive others and yourself for errors.
4. Acceptance of blessings and God's will: You acknowledge the good in your life and accept God's will for your good.
5. Requesting guidance, aid, healing, (and

others) for yourself: You affirm the presence of the solution to any challenge, supply to meet any need, or the reality of a desired condition.

6. Praying for others: You affirm Truth for specific individuals and for the world.

7. Meditation: You spend a few minutes thinking about some divine attribute or quality, such as love, peace, or joy; or you concentrate upon some verse from the Bible or other inspired writing until you feel at one with its meaning.

You can design a seven-step prayer to use for a week, two weeks, a month, or longer. You can retain one or more parts when you write a new seven-step prayer, or you can rewrite all parts. You can change any part at any time. The seven-step prayer is yours, designed by you to fill your prayer needs and to keep your prayers fresh and alive.

The model that is given here shows you what kind of material you might want to use. To design a seven-step prayer, select material for each step—an appropriate affirmation, a short prayer (adapted if you wish), lines from a prayer, psalm or other scriptural passage, or something composed by you; you may use lines from inspirational poems or prose; you may use several items in one section. In the model, some material comes from the Bible and other sources, and some is original.

Seven-Step Prayer Model

1. Illumination: There is but one Presence and one Power in my life, God, the good omniscient. (This is a modification of a statement used in Unity churches.)
   I am now in the presence of pure Being and immersed in the Holy Spirit of life, love, and wisdom. I acknowledge Thy Presence and Thy Power, O blessed Spirit. (Excerpt from an invocation used by Charles Fillmore.)
   All that I think, say, and do this day, I think, say, and do in Thy Presence, by Thy Power, and to Thy glory.

2. Adoration: *Bless the Lord, O my soul; and all that is within me, bless His holy name! Bless the Lord, O my soul, and forget not all his benefits, who forgives all your iniquity, who heals all your diseases, who redeems your life from destruction, who crowns you with lovingkindness and tender mercies, who satisfies you with good as long as you live so that your*

youth is renewed like the eagle's. (Psalms 103:1-5, a blending of the King James and Revised Standard Versions.)

3. Forgiveness: In the name and through the power of Jesus Christ, I accept your forgiveness, Father, remembering Your words spoken through Isaiah: *Remember these things ... for you are my servant; I formed you, you are my servant ... you will not be forgotten by me. I have swept away your transgressions like a cloud, and your sins like mist; return to me, for I have redeemed you.* (Isa. 44:21, 22)

   To all whom I need to forgive, I say in prayer, "There is nothing between us but the love of God. Freely and fully I release all thought of hurt, anger, or resentment. We are at peace, you and I, one in the love of God."

4. Acceptance of blessings and God's will: Father, I gratefully accept the many blessings in my life—health, home, family, friends, good work and the ability and opportunity to do it, abundant supply, and the time to share and enjoy all the good You give. I know that Your will is that I express Your love wherever I am, whatever I do, toward whomever I meet.

Joyfully, I accept Your will as mine. The Twenty-Third Psalm.

5. Requesting guidance, aid, healing, (or others) for myself: The affirmations for oneness, order, and circulation (see page 28).

The Prayer of St. Francis in the affirmative mode (see page 59).

Specific affirmations for fulfillment of specific desires.

6. Praying for others: The Lord's Prayer. Affirmations for specific good for individuals.

An affirmation of world peace, such as: *The peace of God is now established in the minds and hearts of all humankind.*

7. Meditation: ... *God is love, and he who abides in love abides in God, and God abides in him.* (I John 4:16)

Mentally repeat the verse three or more times; then think only the first clause as often as you wish until you feel the truth in it. Sit quietly and let love well up in you. Conclude by mentally repeating the entire verse. Thank God for the realization you have had.

You probably noticed that the seven-step prayer pays attention to our own spiritual needs first. As we move through the first five steps, we rise in or purify our consciousness as our sense of the presence, love, and all-providing power of God becomes stronger. At the end of the fifth step, we should be ready to pray for others with firm conviction.

VI

Prayer Letters

Faithful use of the daily prayer pattern benefits us greatly because the pattern helps keep our conscious thoughts positive and in harmony with the activity of God. We expect good experiences and relationships, speak and act in ways that bring them about, and look for the good that underlies apparently negative situations. Yet, as positively as we may consciously think, speak, and act, we have challenges. Jesus said they would come when He told the disciples: "... *In the world you have tribulation; but be of good cheer, I have overcome the world.*" (John 16:33) Whatever other meaning we can discern in these words, one meaning is that the teachings of Jesus equip His followers to meet successfully the challenges of earthly life. He taught them to deny power to the evil they might encounter and to affirm Truth, God's providing and protecting presence.

Sometimes the "tribulation" in our lives seems to persist no matter how faithfully we affirm Truth. When we have such challenges, we may find that our repeated affirmations keep the thought of the challenge on our minds. If that happens, we might be better advised to write a prayer letter.

There are two kinds of prayer letters: those written to God, and those written to the higher Self or Christ of a person. Both are affirmations written in the form of a letter and "mailed" in the Bible near a passage appropriate to the major concern of the letter.

Whether written to God or to the higher Self of a person, the letter deals not with the problem but with the solution, not with the negative facts but with Truth. The letter acknowledges that the specific good is already present and in the process of manifestation.

Letters to God

Often the challenge that persists is not one that other people would consider serious, but it is serious to the one who is having it. If you find that simply praying positively about the challenge keeps it on your mind, put it in God's hands by writing a letter to Him.

Here is a sample letter that could be written by someone who needs reliable transportation:

Dear God,

You are the source of my supply, and You supply my every need. I know that what is mine by divine right is mine right now. As Your child, I have the right to have reliable transportation so that I may fulfill my obligations as a (worker, student, mother, etc.) and have the freedom to go places for wholesome recreation. The right vehicle at the right price and the funds to pay for it and maintain it properly are available to me at the right time and in the right way.

Thank You, Father, for guidance, inspiration, and Your wise and loving provision for all my needs.

(Your signature)

Among the first letters to God that I ever wrote was a letter very much like this sample. In the process of changing careers, I was trying to live on savings while studying for the ministry. My car had become most unreliable. Repair bills were mounting. The car was worth very little as a trade-in, and I had no extra money for car payments. My prayers seemed to do nothing except keep the problem on my mind, so I wrote a letter, placed it in the Bible at Matthew 6:25-33, the passage in which Jesus tells us not to be anxious about what we need but to seek first the kingdom of God and all that we need will be ours as well. I left the letter in the Bible. Whenever I felt anxiety arising, I reminded myself that I was to seek the kingdom of God, and God would take care of my need. Within less than a month, and at least two months before it was expected, a check refunding my contributions to my retirement fund plus interest arrived. The interest amounted to almost exactly the cash price of the new car I wanted to buy. A man who wanted just the model as my old car purchased it at the price he offered— its trade-in value. Giving thanks for answered prayer, I burned the letter. Since then I have never lacked reliable transportation, and I have written many letters to God.

Letters to God can be written for the fulfillment of any need or desire—to sell a home, find a mate, get a job, resolve a dilemma, and so on. Individuals who have written them report that they, too, quickly cease to worry about how the need or desire is to be fulfilled; they feel assured that it will be, and they quickly recognize what they must do to cooperate with the activity of God to bring what they need or want into manifestation.

A man who felt trapped and helpless in a difficult work situation found that his letter to God reduced stress so he could function in his job while the situation was being resolved. His letter was like the following sample:

Dear God,

I know that You are at work in the situation at the office to bring about order, justice, and harmony. As Your child, I have the right to work under pleasant conditions in which I can be happy and creative. As I remember Your abiding presence, I become a willing channel through which You bring about the right resolution in the right way and at the right time to serve the highest and best inter-

ests of everyone involved in the situation.
   Order, justice, and harmony are now estab-
lished in me and in the situation.
   Thank You, Father.

                           (Signature)

The writer said that he was able to do his own work efficiently and to recognize things he could do to help his co-workers do theirs. He was able to resist efforts made to get him to become involved in the situation and to help certain co-workers remain uninvolved. As a result, the negative aspects of it gradually faded, and a harmonious resolution was achieved.

Letters to Other Persons

Sometimes, if one is involved in a relationship that is stressful, a letter to the higher Self or Christ of the person is more helpful than repeated prayers. Though the prayers may be positive, they can have the effect of keeping one's attention on the difficulty, while a letter to the higher Self of the person can shift one's attention to the Spirit of God within the person. The following sample letter could be written to the higher Self of a co-

worker, neighbor, classmate, or relative who
has exhibited envy and spite:

Dear (person's name),
You are God's beloved, lovable, loving
child, and you express your true nature in all
your relationships, including your relation-
ship with me. You take delight in the good
fortune of others and are sincere in express-
ing congratulations. You are happy and suc-
cessful, so you rejoice when I am happy and
successful.
I see you prosperous, productive, and at
peace within yourself.
(Signature)

Such a letter could be "mailed" in the Bible
near the same passage selected by the writer
of the letter regarding the difficult work
situation, John 13:34, 35—the passage in
which Jesus gave the disciples the command-
ment to love one another as Jesus loved
them.

Individuals who have written letters to the
higher Selves of others say that the change in
their attitude toward the other persons appeared to have an immediate effect. The
writers were able to overlook the negative

words and actions of the other persons and to notice the positive words and actions. As they responded only to the positive words and actions, the other persons ceased to speak and act negatively. In the process, some writers discovered whatever they might have been saying or doing to contribute to the difficulty in their relationships.

In some instances, it is helpful before writing either a letter to God or a letter to the higher Self of a person to write out your actual feelings about the difficult matter. One person calls what is written an "angry letter." It might also be called a "sad letter" or a "frightened letter." Whatever its nature, such a letter lets you empty your mind and heart of thoughts and feelings that can prevent you from having positive thoughts and feelings about the fulfillment of a need or the establishment of a good relationship. The first letter should not be reread after it is written. We do not want to feed negative thoughts and feelings back into our subconscious minds. The letter should be destroyed at once. If possible, the angry, sad, or frightened letter should be burned so that the subconscious mind knows that you are rejecting the thoughts and feelings expressed in it.

After the first letter is destroyed, write the letter to God or to the higher Self of a person.

Methods for Use

There are three commonly used methods for working with prayer letters. Because the function of a prayer letter is to help the writer know the truth about a need, situation, or person, you should use the method which best suits you or the particular challenge, or devise a method of your own. Here are the three most common methods:

Method A
1. Write the letter carefully, being sure to say exactly what you mean to say. Rewrite it as many times as needed to be precise in your word choice.
2. Read the letter, preferably aloud and slowly and thoughtfully, three times just before retiring. Reading it three times impresses the contents on your subconscious mind and alerts it to receive guidance from the superconscious during sleep to pass on to the conscious mind.
3. Giving thanks for answered prayer, place the letter in the Bible near a passage

that is appropriate for the concern and leave it there until the next night at bedtime.

4. Read the letter as in step 2 every night for three weeks. At the end of three weeks, your work is complete; however, most letters are answered before the time is up.

5. At the end of three weeks, you have options: you may burn the letter whether or not the good has appeared; if the good has not appeared, you may leave the letter in the Bible until it does appear or until you feel at peace about the matter. During the extra time, do not read the letter on a regular basis; let Spirit work.

Method B
1. The same as in Method A.
2. The same as in Method A.
3. Place the letter in the Bible as in Method A, but do not reread it unless you feel strongly guided to do so.
4. When you feel right about the matter, whether or not the good has appeared, remove the letter and burn it, giving thanks for answered prayer.

Method C

1. The same as in Method A.
2. The same as in Method A.
3. Place the letter in the Bible as in Method A, giving thanks for answered prayer.
4. The next morning remove the letter from the Bible and burn it, giving thanks that the matter is now in God's hands.

There are many passages in the Bible which are appropriate places to mail prayer letters. For instance, the Twenty-Third Psalm is appropriate for any kind of prayer need. Finding the appropriate place can be as much a part of your receiving the answer to your prayer letter as is the writing of the letter. Sometimes, when a writer finds the best passage in the Bible near which to place a prayer letter, he or she receives the answer.

VII

An Active Denial

As we follow the daily prayer pattern, we have fewer difficulties or challenges because we think, speak, and act in ways that produce them less often, and because we no longer consider certain situations that arise and certain kinds of relationships as challenges. Perhaps we realize that they are powerless over us; perhaps we see that they are no concern of ours; perhaps we simply accept them as part of the milieu in which we live and work.

Often, the challenges that do arise seem quite different from those we previously had. Sometimes they seem to be repetitive or very similar to one another. If that happens to you, and denials and affirmations do not bring relief, you may wish to use a prayer technique designed to cleanse the subconscious memory bank of hidden causes of recurrent challenges.

To Jesus, the cleansing of consciousness was particularly important. Most of His teachings concerning it were given during confrontations with the scribes and Pharisees, the religious leaders of the day. They had great influence, but, said Jesus, their influence was not always beneficial, because what they said and did was polluted by what was in their hearts.

The people of Jesus' day ascribed to the heart what we ascribe to the subconscious phase of mind: to them, the heart was the memory bank and the seat of the feeling nature of man. On one occasion, Jesus said to the scribes, Pharisees, and His disciples: "... *out of the abundance of the heart the mouth speaks. The good man out of his good treasure brings forth good, and the evil man out of his evil treasure brings forth evil.*" (Matt. 12:34, 35) On another occasion, He said: "*Hear and understand: not what goes into the mouth defiles a man, but what comes out of the mouth, this defiles a man. . . . what comes out of the mouth proceeds from the heart, and this defiles a man. For out of the heart come evil thoughts . . . . These are what defile a man . . . .* " (Matt. 15:10, 11, 18-20) On a third occasion, Jesus burst into rather strong words when He said: *"Woe to you, scribes and Pharisees, hypocrites! for you cleanse the outside of the cup and of the plate, but inside they are full of extortion and rapacity. You blind Pharisee! first cleanse the inside of the cup and of the plate, that the outside also may be clean."* (Matt. 23:25) Jesus was not giving instructions for dishwashing. If He were, they were poor instructions, because cleaning the inside of a utensil does not automatically cleanse the outside. Jesus was using a familiar image to teach that we can and must cleanse our minds of anything which causes us to say words or perform acts which are harmful to ourselves and others. Because He used the word *heart* so often, we know that He was as much concerned about the cleansing of the subconscious mind as the conscious mind.

But cleansing of the subconscious mind must be handled carefully. In a parable told to the scribes and Pharisees, Jesus taught that when we cleanse our minds of harmful thoughts, feelings, beliefs, and attitudes, we must immediately replace them with beneficial thoughts, feelings, beliefs, and attitudes.

If we do not, we may have simply prepared the way for even more harmful thoughts, feelings, beliefs, and attitudes to take over our minds. The parable is recorded in the Gospel According to Matthew:

"When the unclean spirit has gone out of a man, he passes through waterless places seeking rest, but he finds none. Then he says, 'I will return to my house from which I came.' And when he comes he finds it empty, swept, and put in order. Then he goes and brings with him seven other spirits more evil than himself, and they enter and dwell there; and the last state of that man becomes worse than the first....
(Matt. 12:43-45)

The *unclean spirit* is, of course, a thought, feeling, belief, or attitude that spoils our lives in some way. The house represents the individual consciousness. We know that we can use denials to cleanse our minds. So, by implication, Jesus was teaching that denials must immediately be followed by affirmations. Though the practice of using denials will help us to cleanse our conscious minds of recognizably harmful thoughts, feelings, beliefs, and attitudes, often the unclean spirits that cause the most trouble are hidden in the basements of our houses of consciousness—in the subconscious memory banks. Not all the troublemakers are by nature harmful; many are simply no longer appropriate; but because they still form the hidden motives for conscious thoughts, words, and deeds, they spoil our experience. For instance, a child needs to learn not to play with matches; but an adult must know how to strike them. If the early learning makes the adult afraid to strike matches, an inappropriate thought is spoiling the adult's life.

Today, many physicians and medical researchers report a relationship between specific kinds of ailments and diseases and specific thoughts, feelings, beliefs, and attitudes, both conscious and unconscious. Indeed, physicians and researchers agree that the unconscious ones—those connected with repressed or deeply buried memories—seem to have the most devastating effect upon health. What is *in the heart* can apparently disorder our biochemistry and actually bring on major health problems. Certainly, psychologists and psychiatrists have discovered that what is *in the heart* can make individuals accident-prone, alcoholic, chronically unlucky in love, afraid of success, irrationally suspicious of other persons, self-distrustful, painfully shy, obsessive, or depressed, to name but a few undesirable conditions. If what is *in the heart* is negative or inappropriate, it will eventually defile a person's own life in some way and also the lives of his or her close associates.

Metaphysicians believe that the subconscious phase of mind is the seat of the intuitive faculty which channels divine guidance to the conscious mind. Whether or not the belief is justified, practitioners of positive prayer find that as they cleanse the memory bank of inappropriate and negative thoughts, feelings, beliefs, and attitudes, their prayers become more productive, as if they had cleared obstructions from the channel of intuition so that divine ideas flow freely into their minds.

There is a positive prayer technique which has helped numerous individuals overcome recurrent challenges of all kinds that arise from deeply buried memories. Since first devised in the present form, it has been taught to more than a thousand individuals in classes and counseling sessions and to patients with persistent psychological or physical problems.

A Burning

The technique is an active denial called "A Burning" because it combines written, spoken, and silent affirmations with the use of fire to impress the subconscious mind with the individual's power to dispose of thoughts, feelings, beliefs, and attitudes underlying some persistent challenge. Long associated in race mind with cleansing and refining, fire makes a strong impression on the subconscious mind. In addition, fire is known to be the visible aspect of a process by which collected energy is released to produce light and heat.

Energy is the name given to the invisible but basic material stuff of the universe. It collects in subatomic particles, holds particles together to form atoms, holds atoms together to form molecules, and so on up the chain of matter until the collected energy forms minerals, plants, and the bodies of animals and man. Energy vibrates; it is constantly in motion even when collected into apparently solid, unmoving forms. Everything is made of energy, and everything emits some energy. Our bodies, which are made of energy, emit energy. Even our thoughts and feelings are patterns of energy, and the energy they emit can actually make patterns on graphs. Beliefs and attitudes are habitual thoughts that have feelings attached to them. A past event that was so disturbing as to be deliberately buried in the memory bank usually was buried because it aroused a strong feeling called an *emotion,* considered dangerous because if expressed it could lead the individual to perform some forbidden action.

According to the dictionary, an emotion is *any departure from the usual calm state of the organism as includes strong feeling, an impulse to overt action, and internal bodily changes in respiration, circulation, glandular action, etc.* Since an emotion prepares the human body to release energy through overt action, if the energy is not released, it is trapped with the memory of the event which aroused the emotion. But the nature of energy is to move, and some of the emotional energy tends to be emitted whenever there seems to be an appropriate moment. It is safe to assume that anyone who has not deliberately cleansed his or her memory bank of suppressed memories has a large store of trapped thought energy and emotional energy buried deep in the subconscious mind. Whenever an event occurs that is in some way similar to some buried memory, some trapped thought energy and emotional energy may escape to disrupt normal bodily functions or perhaps cause inappropriate or overreactive behavior.

To deal with most challenges, a spoken or silent denial followed by an appropriate affirmation is effective; but when we do not know what specific thought, feeling, belief, or attitude needs to be denied, the burning technique can be helpful. It is a safe, quick, and practical way to release trapped mental or emotional energy and, at the same time, issue new orders that contradict previous orders to the subconscious mind.

The subconscious mind has been compared to an obedient but not very bright servant whose principal function is to keep its master alive, safe, and (in its master's conception of happiness) happy. From the moment we are born, we issue orders to our servant, first as feelings, and then, when we have them, as words. When we order the servant to bury an unpleasant memory, we do it with a feeling or a thought that means, "I never want to think of this again." We issue such orders even when we are babies; indeed, persons who conduct burnings often find that buried causes of recurrent challenges are the thoughts, feelings, beliefs, or attitudes connected with incidents from their infancy. Sometimes the memories which surface during a burning are not of actual events but of frightening stories or plays which aroused disturbing thoughts or feelings. It makes no difference whether the memories are of actual or fictitious events, if the person orders the subconscious mind to bury the memories, the emotional energy and the energy of the thoughts, feelings, beliefs, and attitudes trapped with them can be disruptive and can interfere with the reception of right answers to prayers.

Fortunately, your subconscious mind will respond to your conscious commands; but you need to be firm in your purpose. If your present conscious intention wavers, the subconscious mind will continue to do whatever you have commanded it to do in the past.

To conduct a burning, you need a suitable place or container such as a fireplace, large ashtray, hibachi, barbecue pit, metal bucket, or even a metal kitchen sink. You also need several sheets of paper and a pen or pencil.

It is best to do a burning when you know you will be uninterrupted for an hour or more.

Since a burning typically releases energy, it is also best to do it between four and six hours before bedtime; if you do a burning too late at night, you may find yourself awake until dawn. Incidentally, a burning is a private matter. If anyone else is present, be sure that the person will take the process seriously and give psychological and spiritual support to your purpose.

Instructions

Here are the steps to follow:

1. Begin by affirming the presence of God. You may use any affirmation you wish, but it is important that you repeat it at least three times to impress it upon your subconscious mind.

2. Next, affirm that since God is present, memories are powerless to disturb or harm you. It is important that you tell your subconscious mind that you want it to reveal memories to you and that you feel perfectly safe.

3. *Declare aloud: I now release the thoughts, feelings, beliefs, and attitudes that are causing* _____ .
Fill in the blank with a phrase describing the

challenge. For instance, the phrase might be *frequent colds, persistent depression, chronic loneliness, irrational anger, fear of failure, fear of success, sense of unworthiness, symptoms of (some ailment),* or *accident proneness.*

If you wish, tell your subconscious mind to reveal the memories. Speak to it as if it is an obedient servant of which you are very fond. Say: *You are now to reveal the memories attached to the thoughts, feelings, beliefs, and attitudes that are causing* _____ .

4. Head the first sheet of paper with these words: *I now release these errors; I loose them; I let them go; and I let God have His perfect way with them.* The errors are the thoughts, feelings, beliefs, and attitudes attached to the memories. The memories are not errors; whether of actual or fictitious events, they are a part of your past experience, and they were recorded as you interpreted them. Even if you now recognize that your interpretation was a distortion, the distortion itself is a valid part of your past. The error lies in holding on to the particular thoughts, feelings, beliefs, and attitudes.

5. Sit quietly, and in a short time, memories will begin to surface. Write down, preferably in short phrases, the thoughts, feelings,

beliefs, or attitudes attached to the memories. Do not write down the events, and do not reread what you write. Use a clean sheet of paper to cover each phrase as you complete it. Reading back what you write will tend to feed the phrases back into the memory bank. Do not censor anything that comes. It does not matter if you see no connection between your challenge and the memories that come. At the time the events occurred, each seemed to confirm some thought, feeling, belief, or attitude about yourself, other persons, or the world, and your obedient subconscious servant filed them away with other memories that seemed related. You may see nothing negative about some memory or the thought, feeling, belief, or attitude accompanying it; write it down anyway. Remember, something that was positive in the past can be inappropriate in the present.

A woman counselee gave me permission to use her experience as an example. Her burning was conducted to eliminate the thoughts, feelings, beliefs, and attitudes that caused her inability to form lasting friendships. Repeatedly, individuals she valued stopped including her in parties, had previous engagements when she wanted to see them, became too busy to call or write. When she did her burning, she saw many incidents from her childhood and adolescence in which she was being helpful. Her sheets of paper were filled with words such as these: "Being liked for being helpful"; "feeling good about me because I helped"; "helpfulness means love"; "love means helpfulness." It was as if a file drawer marked "How I Can Get People To Like Me" had been dumped for her to inspect. She said that she was puzzled, but she moved through all the steps of the burning, and when it was over, she received a revelation. Behavior learned in childhood and adolescence had caused her to become compulsively helpful so that as an adult she smothered others with her helpfulness. Her belief led to inappropriate behavior with adults who simply wanted her companionship.

Often, however, there are recognizably negative thoughts, feelings, beliefs, and attitudes attached to the revealed memories, such as fear of the dark, anger at being teased, jealousy of someone, suspicion of people who are nice to me, terror of being dropped. We need to use any means we can to release the energy of such thoughts.

6. When no more memories come, turn

the pages over so that you cannot read what you have written, and tear them to shreds, repeating aloud: *I now release these errors; I loose them; I let them go; and I let God have His perfect way with them.*

7. Now begin to burn the shreds of paper, and as they burn, watch the flames and declare aloud: *Divine Love consumes these errors. The energy is released to be reused in a new and better form.* Repeat the affirmation as long as the burning continues. You may burn one scrap of paper at a time, or several. If the scraps burn at different rates, that is all right. Reduce all paper to ashes.

8. When the paper is reduced to ashes, say a prayer of thanksgiving for your freedom from the errors of the past. You might want to use this prayer: "Thank You, God, for my freedom from the mistakes of the past and the results of the mistakes of the past."

9. Immediately, use an affirmation that claims the good that had seemed to be blocked by the thoughts, feelings, beliefs, and attitudes which you have just burned. The woman mentioned in Step 5 used this affirmation: *I now attract and enjoy lasting friendships.* As soon as she received the revelation about herself, she used this affirma-

tion: *My friends enjoy my company and like me for myself alone.*

This step is important because you do not wish to prepare clean living quarters for "*... seven other spirits more evil...*" (Matt. 12:45) than the ones you have just ousted.

10. When the burning is over, simply go about your business. If thoughts about the burned material come back, gently dismiss them. Tell them that they have served their purpose in your life and that they may now leave. Even the negative thoughts, feelings, beliefs, and attitudes have probably served some valuable purpose. Fear of the dark, for instance, may have kept you as a child from going into dangerous places, or suspicion of people who were nice to you may have protected you from dangerous strangers. As soon as you dismiss the thought, tell your subconscious servant: *I have no more need for that thought. Deactivate it and release the energy.*

11. Replace the dismissed thought with a positive statement such as: *I am poised and centered in the (peace, love, joy, forgiveness, security, strength, beauty, success, etc.) of God. The _____ in my soul is undisturbed by anyone or any circumstance,*

past or present. Choose a word that is the antidote for the negative or inappropriate thought, feeling, belief, or attitude.

12. Generally, all thoughts of the past dissipate quickly. Occasionally, one persists for two or three days. If that happens, it is a signal that there is another "file drawer" that needs to be emptied. Conduct a second burning if needed. After all, you did command the subconscious servant to release whatever was causing some specific challenge, and it is dutifully trying to get your cooperation. In the second burning, focus on the persistent thought. Say: *I now release the thoughts, feelings, beliefs, and attitudes that are causing me to remember (the time I lost the race or my third birthday party or the fight with my cousin).* Go through all the steps as you did for the first burning. A third burning may even be necessary.

Mental Burnings

After you have done a few burnings, you will probably find that you can do burnings mentally by issuing orders to your subconscious servant with words such as these: *Now release the thoughts, feelings, beliefs, and attitudes that are causing (this challenge) and burn them.* You may or may not be aware of specific memories or thoughts when you do a mental burning. It does not matter. The subconscious servant will simply do as you say. Some persons who have performed mental burnings report that they sometimes get a sensation of warmth. Most persons say that in a day or so, they remember some long forgotten incident, but that it has no power to disturb them.

Whether you perform an actual or a mental burning, the process clears your total consciousness of whatever has blocked some form of your good. After a burning, if the complete resolution of the challenge for which you did the burning requires you to take action, you will receive definite ideas to help you. God is always active to provide for the welfare of His creation. As soon as we clear the channel which connects our conscious minds with God-Mind, we receive ideas that help us claim the good that God has provided.

VIII

Scriptural Affirmations

Whether we cleanse our consciousness by using only denials or by using the burning technique, we need to fill our minds immediately with affirmations of Truth that contradict the erroneous, negative, or inappropriate thoughts, feelings, beliefs, and attitudes that have been released. They formed the basis for habits of speech and action which have in some way hindered our acceptance of the health, happiness, harmonious relationships, prosperity, and peace of mind that we, as offspring of God, should experience. Unless we consciously work to form new mental habits in harmony with God's good will for us, the old habits will reassert themselves.

The Bible is full of affirmative statements

on almost every subject; and since earliest times, people have used scriptural statements to keep their minds focused upon the goodness of God's will for humanity. Various characters in the Old Testament, including the prophets, quoted scriptural passages to keep their minds focused, and so did Jesus and Paul and other writers of the New Testament.

There is a positive prayer technique for using scriptural affirmations that has helped numerous individuals form new mental habits strong enough to overcome the old habits which have spoiled their lives. This same technique can be used simply to improve the quality of one's life or to stimulate one's spiritual growth.

Here are the steps:

1. Find verses in the Bible which assure you that God supplies the good you desire. To find the verses easily, look up the key word in the concordance. If you do not own a concordance, you can find one in the reference section of your local public library. Look up the references in your own Bible and copy by hand on small cards (3x5 index cards are a convenient size) the verses that most appeal to you; put only one verse on each side of a

card. The good work of this technique actually begins with the choosing of the verses and the copying of them by hand, for these acts impress the subconscious mind with the truths you want to remember. You may select as many verses as you wish.

To clarify the above instructions, let us suppose that a man has suffered for a long time from persistent low-back pain for which doctors have found no physical cause. He has had temporary relief from medications, but he wants to be free of pain without depending upon drugs, and he wants to have a dependably strong back. Let us further suppose that he does a burning and the pain disappears, but in a few days he finds himself wondering when he will have another attack of low-back pain. He needs to focus on his own God-given strength, so he looks up the word *strength* in the concordance and, among the 300 or more verses that deal with strength and related words, he finds many that appeal to him. Let us say he chooses these: *"The Lord is my strength and my song...."* (Exod. 15:2) *"This God is my strong refuge, and has made my way safe."* (II Sam. 22:33) *I love thee, O Lord, my strength.* (Psalms 18:1) ... *The Lord is the stronghold of my life; of whom shall I be afraid?* (Psalms 27:1) *The Lord is my strength and my shield; in him my heart trusts; so I am helped, and my heart exults, and with my song I give thanks to him.* (Psalms 28:7) ... *be strong in the Lord and in the strength of his might.* (Eph. 6:10) *I can do all things in him who strengthens me.* (Phil. 4:13) ... *the Lord stood by me and gave me strength....* (II Tim. 4:17)

The man in our example writes the verses on four cards, putting only one verse on each side.

2. That night, and every night that you use this technique, give thanks for answered prayer, and just before retiring, slowly and thoughtfully read each verse. In the morning, during your first prayer time, give thanks for answered prayer, and read the verses again.

3. Carry the cards with you wherever you go during the day, and read one at random whenever you have idle-thought time (as in step 6 of the daily prayer pattern) and consider its meaning. As you return the card to your pocket or handbag, thank God for your ability to believe the truth of the passage.

4. As soon as you think that you really believe the truth in the verses, visualize yourself with the challenge overcome. The man

with the low-back pain might see himself lifting heavy objects with complete freedom and ease. A person needing money to repair the roof might see herself handing a check to a workman. Do the visualization several times a day, particularly when you have been contemplating one of the verses.

5. If you wish, when you feel that belief is firmly established, set a reasonable date for the resolution of the challenge. If you set a date, be bold and circle it on the calendar, and make a declaration such as this: *By this date, my good will come to me.* Often, persons who feel impelled to set a date also receive definite guidance to do some specific thing. It is important to follow the guidance because God works through us to provide whatever good we seek.

6. Although you have thanked God every time you have read the cards, at the first outward sign of the resolution of the challenge, give special thanks. For the man with the fear that low-back pain might return, a sign of resolution could be that he has spent a whole day without once worrying about the pain.

7. As soon as you feel satisfied that the spiritual progress is complete, discontinue regular use of the scriptural affirmations.

Persons who have circled a date on the calendar usually feel that, even though the good they seek has not yet completely materialized, the process is complete on the circled date. From then on, whenever you think about the challenge, simply thank God for the perfect resolution. You might also add: *I have placed this matter in the hands of God.*

The time one needs to spend working with the scriptural affirmation technique is an individual matter. Psychologists say that three weeks is the time required to form a new habit; so for most persons, particularly those to whom deliberate prayer work is new, it is advisable to devote at least three weeks to the scriptural affirmation technique. If during the time the original verses lose their freshness, feel free to find new ones. Persons experienced in prayer often have the results they seek in less than three weeks; but even among them, some have spent much longer periods to overcome long-standing challenges. One of my counselees had almost instantaneous results. She spent about two hours looking for and copying appropriate verses to help her overcome the challenge of irrational fear. During her evening prayer time, she contemplated the verses. The next morning she awoke with the feeling that the work was done; and it was. She has been free of irrational fear ever since.

Whether or not you have a specific challenge to overcome, the scriptural affirmation technique is valuable. Many persons seeking spiritual growth use it to stimulate a particular spiritual attribute such as faith, order, love, will, understanding, judgment, imagination, power, forgiveness, life, strength (for which a few verses have already been supplied), or zeal. Others use the technique solely to give themselves inspirational material to contemplate during idle-thought time. Whether you are using the technique to overcome a challenge, for spiritual growth, or simply for inspiration, scriptural affirmations will supply you with the means to make step six of the daily prayer pattern into a life-changing activity.

IX

Visualization As Prayer

As you have noticed, positive prayer often calls for visualization—the formation of mental pictures or images of good things or conditions not yet present in the material world. Mental pictures reinforce the intention to claim good which we declare with prayers and affirmations. If our memory banks hold mental pictures which conflict with our affirmations, the mental pictures can neutralize the affirmations; but we can consciously neutralize the effect of the old mental pictures by deliberately forming new ones and constantly thinking about them.

We can all deliberately visualize or imagine things, conditions, and actions; but if we were not encouraged to use that ability when we were youngsters, we may have to train ourselves to use it now. It is well worth the effort, because visualization is useful not only for prayer but for many other activities. It is used by athletes and performing artists to improve their skills; by directors of drama and dance to plan productions; by architects to design buildings; by engineers to plan bridges; by carpenters to execute blueprints; by surgeons to plan operations; by sales representatives to make good impressions on prospects. In fact, visualization is used by just about anyone who wishes to do something well, from giving a party to passing a driving test or performing well in an oral examination.

For several years visualization has been prescribed for patients undergoing medical treatment for certain kinds of cancer, and many patients who have used it have been healed. The same technique has helped speed the healing of broken bones or injured muscles and helped countless overweight patients lose unwanted pounds.

Two Training Exercises

If you have difficulty deliberately making mental pictures, you can stimulate your imagination by setting aside ten minutes a day for two or three weeks to practice two simple exercises.

Exercise 1

1. Select an object such as a colored ball or patterned dish or a flower.

2. Look at the object, carefully noting its size, shape, color or colors, and anything else distinctive about it.

3. Now close your eyes and describe it to yourself in detail.

4. Then declare that the object is now forming on a mental screen, and turn your attention inward. Sit quietly for a few seconds to allow the object to form.

5. If you do not see the object mentally in a few seconds, open your eyes and look at the actual object again; then close your eyes and repeat the process. Usually, only a few attempts are needed to trigger the mental picture-making mechanism.

7. If you continue to have difficulty, simply describe to yourself what you wish to see. After a few days, the faithful servant in your subconscious mind will activate your faculty of imagination.

This exercise should be done for several days until the mental pictures are clear. Use a different object each day. If you wish, you can use two or three objects during one session. Most people find that the picture-making mechanism is in good running order in a week to ten days.

As soon as you can visualize objects clearly, go on to the second exercise which is designed to help you see things and people in motion.

Exercise 2

1. Turn on the television set and watch the action with the sound turned off.
2. Close your eyes and declare that the action is now replaying on your mental screen, and turn your attention inward. Sit quietly for a few seconds to allow the picture to form, and watch the action.
3. If you do not see the mental motion picture in a few seconds, open your eyes and look at the action on the television screen. Of course, it will not be the same, but that does not matter. You are really just telling your subconscious mind to activate the mental picture-making mechanism to form

images in motion.

4. Close your eyes again and declare that the action you have just seen is now replaying on your mental screen, and turn your attention inward. Usually, only a few attempts are needed before you see the replay.

5. After the first time you have clearly seen the replay, do the exercise for at least three more sessions.

Once you have the picture-making mechanism in good running order, it is wise to spend a few minutes each day doing visualization. To make those minutes valuable, try visualizing beautiful places you have seen or happy memories you have had. Then try visualizing yourself doing things you have always wanted to do but have not done—sailing a boat, skiing, dancing modern ballet. As you do this kind of visualization, you are likely to feel the action, for it is not uncommon for this kind of visualization to be accompanied by kinesthesia—the sense of bodily activity. Apparently, the subconscious mind responds to mental pictures by stimulating appropriate muscles or internal organs.

Visualization with kinesthesia is useful for healing. For instance, suppose a man has injured his ankle and has had medical treatment for it but has decided also to use positive prayer techniques to speed the healing. He might affirm that the activity of God is restoring the ankle to its normal state, and then he might visualize it as healed. Next, he might imagine himself walking normally, running, and perhaps climbing stairs or dancing. As he visualized the actions, he would probably become aware of some muscular sensations even though the ankle was not moving. Visualization of this kind is not only harmless, it is actually beneficial. It is the kind of visualization people have used for centuries to improve skills when they are not outwardly practicing them.

Often, when used to help overcome health challenges, visualization may involve rather fanciful images, because no one really knows what occurs during the healing process. A woman suffering from old adhesions from previous abdominal surgery used the affirmation: *Father, I give thanks that my abdominal organs are free to function without restrictions.* Then she visualized cobwebs being gently brushed away from the walls and pillars in a cavernous hall. She did the visualization for a few minutes several times a day.

In a little more than a week, all symptoms of adhesions disappeared.

When to Visualize

Visualization can be done anytime and anywhere; but as a positive prayer technique, it is most effective when one is in a relaxed, rather drowsy state. In a drowsy state, the conscious mind is almost inactive and the subconscious mind can follow the few directions that the conscious mind gives without being interrupted by extraneous thoughts. So, an ideal time to use visualization as prayer is just before you go to sleep. The process is simple.

1. Begin with an appropriate affirmation to claim the good you desire. Suppose you want harmony with a coworker. Your affirmation might be: *Father, I give thanks that Mary and I now work together in harmony.*

2. Then visualize yourself with the prayer answered. You see or feel yourself in an imaginary scene in which you and Mary are happily performing a task together, a scene that has not taken place recently or perhaps has never taken place. Were you in a completely alert state, your conscious mind

might not let the picture form since it is contrary to fact; but with the conscious mind almost at rest, the subconscious mind can accept the imaginary scene and prepare to channel ideas to your conscious mind, which will help you to make such a scene materialize.

3. When you feel satisfied with the visualization, thank God for answered prayer. Should you fall asleep with the imaginary scene still on your mental screen, your subconscious mind will continue to hold it. Persons who have fallen asleep during visualization report that when they awaken they usually know exactly what they need to do to help make the imaginary scene an actuality. Then thank God for answered prayer and follow the guidance as soon as possible.

If you wish to use visualization as prayer during the day or when you are not feeling sleepy, you can induce a drowsy state with a relaxation technique.

Relaxation Techniques

The following relaxation techniques combine visualization as prayer with relaxation methods taught by physicians, psychologists, and biofeedback trainers. If you have no specific prayer request and simply want to relax, you can use only the steps in either technique that are designed to relax the body. Some individuals have recorded the instructions on tape.

1. Lie on your back on a bed or on the floor, and make your prayer request.

2. Close your eyes and take a few deep breaths, saying silently to your lungs with each exhalation: *My lungs are free and relaxed.* Breathe normally.

3. Turn your attention to your legs and say to them silently several times: *My legs are warm and heavy and relaxed.* Let them sink into the surface on which you are lying.

4. When your legs feel relaxed, speak to your arms, saying silently: *My arms are warm and heavy and relaxed.* Let them sink into the surface on which you are lying.

5. When your arms are relaxed, speak to your hips, saying silently: *My hips are warm and heavy and relaxed.* Let them sink into the surface on which you are lying.

6. When your hips are relaxed, speak to

your entire spine, saying silently: *My spine is warm and heavy and relaxed.* Let it sink into the surface on which you are lying.

7. When your spine is relaxed, if you feel any tension in your abdomen, speak to it, saying silently: *My abdomen is warm and heavy and relaxed.*

8. When your abdomen is relaxed, if you feel any tension in your neck and throat, speak to them, saying silently: *My neck and throat are warm and heavy and relaxed.*

9. When your neck and throat are relaxed, if you feel any tension in your scalp and forehead, speak to them, saying silently: *My scalp and forehead are warm and heavy and relaxed.*

10. When your scalp and forehead are relaxed, speak to your eyelids, saying silently: *My eyelids are warm and heavy and relaxed.*

11. When your whole physical being feels relaxed, slowly think: *I am relaxed,* each time you exhale.

12. When you begin to feel drowsy, start your visualization.

13. At the end of the visualization, thank God for answered prayer.

14. Lie quietly for a few minutes before resuming your usual activities.

If you prefer, you can do the above relaxation technique sitting in a comfortable chair, preferably one into which your body seems to sink.

The following technique may also be done either lying down or sitting in a comfortable chair.

1. Make your prayer request.

2. Close your eyes and notice your breathing. Do not adjust it; just notice how the air feels in your nostrils as you inhale and exhale for ten complete breaths.

3. As you inhale, feel the air in your nostrils; and as you exhale, think the word *God* or *peace* or any one-syllable word that induces a sense of inner quiet.

3. Continue this until you feel drowsy, and then begin your visualization.

5. At the end of the visualization, thank God for answered prayer.

6. Lie or sit quietly for a few minutes before resuming your usual activities.

If several times a week for a month or so you practice either of these relaxation techniques or any other that you prefer, you may not need to use one to induce a relaxed, drowsy state; for you will have conditioned your subconscious mind to relax your body and eyelids on command, and you will have disciplined your conscious mind to slow down, stop thinking extraneous thoughts, and focus on prayer and visualization.

Visualization with Color and Light

You need not always focus on scenes or actions to make effective use of visualization in prayer. You can simply focus on light of different colors. There are two reasons for the effectiveness of visualizing light and color: (1) light and color are the visual effects of energy vibrating at specific rates; (2) each color has various symbolic meanings which are recorded in race mind and are therefore available to our individual subconscious minds, whether or not we consciously know about color symbolism.

Color symbolism must be as ancient as the use of color itself. Anthropologists and archaeologists have identified the symbolic use of color in artifacts of various kinds. Egyptologists recognize many symbolic meanings in the colors used in tomb decorations and paintings.

Color apparently had symbolic meaning for the ancient Jews. When color is mentioned in the Old Testament, it seems to have great significance. For instance, in the twenty-fifth through twenty-eighth chapters of Exodus, God instructed Moses to build a tabernacle and told him exactly what colors to use for the tent, the loops of the curtains, the veil, and the screen—blue, purple, and scarlet. He also told Moses to use gold, silver, and bronze for various metallic parts of the sanctuary and to have cloth made of gold, blue, purple, and scarlet for the priests' garments.

Interestingly, these same colors appear in the religious objects and clothing used in diverse cultures. Apparently, the symbolism of color is imprinted on what the great Swiss psychologist C. G. Jung called the universal unconscious, and what metaphysicians call race mind; for, among various peoples there are great similarities in the meanings ascribed to particular colors. During the Middle Ages and Renaissance in Europe few people could read, so Christian artists used the symbolism of color to convey the meaning of any scene they depicted in colored glass or paintings. Simply by observing the clothing of depicted persons, an illiterate peasant knew that the one clothed in clear blue was godly, while the one clothed in black was ungodly.

Today, designers of dramatic productions for stage, screen, and television employ color symbolism much as those artists did. Every child knows that the "good guy wears a white hat" and the "bad guy wears a black hat." Of course, color symbolism is used in school emblems, flags of nations, and the colors associated with certain holidays.

Probably, if one has spontaneous mental pictures in color when awake, or one dreams in color, the colors have meanings, because the subconscious mind, always directly connected with race mind, knows the meanings of colors and could well be using them to convey information about the individual's inner state. Obviously, knowledge of color symbolism could be helpful in interpreting dreams for gaining self-understanding.

To assist you in reading the symbolism of colors, a list of the most common meanings follows. The meanings come from a variety of sources, including the writings of the Greek philosopher Pythagoras, who lived during the 6th century B.C., and the mystical teachings of the Jews contained in the Cabala, which as oral tradition may date back to the time of

Moses but more certainly was extant in the 3d century B.C.; however, only the meanings used by the Christian church have been specifically identified. Unless otherwise noted, the colors mentioned are the clear, definite hues.

Color Symbolism List

Red: Life, vitality, force, body, underworld. Christian church: suffering and death of Jesus Christ and the saints, divine love, blood.

Dark Red: Christian church: warfare and human suffering.

Muddy Red: Rage.

Orange: Enthusiasm, intuition, energy.

Yellow: Good judgment or wisdom, intelligence, mind, Earth.

Gold: Understanding. Christian church: glory, fruitfulness, divine wisdom.

Green: Order, health, healing. Christian church: fertility (hence, prosperity).

Spring Green: Strength. Christian church: youthfulness.

Blue: Faith, spirit of man. Christian church: heaven, godliness, (hence, divine love in man.)

Light Blue: Imagination.
Violet: Christian church: humility, deep affection, sorrow, spiritual gifts.
Purple: Power. (This color was reserved for rulers in ancient times because the dye was expensive and so the color became associated with power.)
Pink: Love, human affection.
Russet: Purification (presumably from the color of leaves in the fall).
Gray: Will.
White: Pure spirit. Christian church: purity, innocence, light, joy, the Christ, God.
Black: Christian church: death, destruction, ungodliness.

Because the answer to prayer is often given in a dream or a waking vision that is in color, knowledge of the meanings of colors can help a person understand the answer.

Recently, attention has been paid to the psychological effects of color. A serious study showed that exposure to the color pink seems to reduce muscle tension and combativeness in violent or hostile persons. Certainly, most individuals have favorite colors which they say make them feel good and some colors which they say depress them.

For many years, physicians and psychologists have studied the relationship between color preferences and personality characteristics and have occasionally used color as a therapeutic tool.

There is mounting contemporary evidence that a long-standing claim of metaphysicians is valid—color can have significance for healing. Some present-day holistic healers employ specific colors of light to alleviate or heal specific ailments.

The practitioner of positive prayer need not study the therapeutic effects of specific colors, however, because the individual's own subconscious mind is under the direction of superconscious mind and can be trusted to select whatever color will help a specific condition. Color, remember, is simply the visual effect of energy vibrating at a particular rate. Your subconscious mind will select the vibratory rate needed to tone up any specific organ so that it will function at the healthy rate for it.

Here is a light drill which many practitioners of positive prayer believe has helped them keep their physical bodies healthy or restored their bodies to health. It begins with visualizing white light because (as sunlight passed through a prism reveals) white light contains all colors.

Light Drill

1. Sit with your spine straight, or lie flat on the floor or a bed and, if necessary, do a relaxation exercise.

2. Affirm: *I thank You, God, for Your healing power which flows through me now as light, renewing and restoring every part of my body.*

3. Inhale deeply, imagining white light entering through the top of your head and filling your head.

4. Hold your breath, imagining white light traveling throughout your body and all the way to your fingers and toes.

5. Exhale, imagining the light radiating from every pore or changing to bluish-gray, which, according to persons who can see the energy field emitted by and surrounding human bodies, is the normal color of the health aura.

6. Repeat steps 3, 4, and 5 using each color of the spectrum in the following order: red, orange, yellow, green, blue, purple (or

indigo), violet. Be sure you visualize clear, definite hues.

7. Repeat steps 3, 4, and 5 using white light again.

8. Affirm: *Thank You, God, for renewing and restoring every part of my body.* Sit or lie quietly for a minute or two.

You may prefer, particularly if you are enjoying vigorous health, to use only the first 5 steps and concentrate on the white light; if so, repeat steps 3, 4, and 5 three times and close with the affirmation.

If, when you are doing the complete light drill, one color seems to linger in a specific body area, use that color twice more and concentrate it in the area before moving on to the next color.

Light Drill Modification

The light drill can be modified to stimulate specific attributes of character or mind which you might wish to develop. Let us suppose that you wish to become more enthusiastic. Here is how to modify the light drill for that purpose.

1. Sit with your spine straight, or lie flat

on the floor or a bed and, if necessary, do a relaxation exercise.

2. Affirm: *I thank You, God, for increasing my capacity for enthusiasm.*

3. Inhale deeply, imagining white light entering through the top of your head and filling your head.

4. Hold your breath, imagining white light traveling throughout your body and all the way to your fingers and toes.

5. Exhale, imagining the light radiating from every pore and enveloping you and radiating outward in all directions.

6. Repeat steps 3, 4, and 5 using orange light (which symbolizes enthusiasm) or the color you associate with the attribute.

7. Repeat steps 3, 4, and 5 using white light again.

8. Affirm: *Thank You, God, for filling me with enthusiasm.* Sit or lie quietly for a minute or two.

Of course, the light drill can be used to assist healing, whether or not you are under the care of a physician. Several individuals who have consulted me for spiritual help have sped the healing of broken bones by using the light drill and visualizing the light stitching the specific bone together. Their physicians have expressed amazement at their rapid recovery.

Visualization and Forgiveness

As spiritual teachers have pointed out for a long time, and the medical profession is now recognizing, a correlation exists between our mental and physical states. The negative thoughts and feelings associated with the mental state of unforgiveness have deleterious effects upon our physical bodies. But we are not always aware that we are harboring unforgiving thoughts and feelings because many of them may be buried in the subconscious memory bank. A burning can release them. But whether or not we do a burning, we can use a positive prayer technique that combines visualization of light in an affected body area with release of unforgiving thoughts and feelings. If you wish to use this technique in conjunction with medical treatment, use it morning and evening until the healing takes place. If the condition has confined you to bed, you may wish to use the technique every two or three hours that you are awake until you feel that the healing has taken place. This technique has also been used by healthy persons once a month as preventive spiritual medicine.

Since a person usually needs to spend about a quarter of an hour to complete the steps of this technique, it has been given a name.

The Fifteen-Minute Treatment

1. Assume a comfortable, relaxed position, either sitting or lying down.

2. Affirm three times, aloud or silently, resting quietly a few moments between declarations: *God is the life within me.*

3. Affirm three times, aloud or silently, resting quietly a few moments between declarations: *I now release every recognized or unrecognized feeling of fear, resentment, condemnation, envy, distrust, hate, or any other negative feeling or thought about myself or anything I may have said, thought, or done. I forgive myself for everything, and I love and bless myself.*

4. Affirm three times, aloud or silently, resting quietly a few moments between declarations: *Divine love now dissolves and dissipates every wrong condition in my*

mind, body, and relationships.

5. Now visualize in detail and in color the most beautiful, peaceful scene you can. Bring all your senses to play, and let the feeling of complete oneness with God and the universe fill your being. Feel yourself melting into the scene.

6. Gradually let the feeling become light that is going through your circulatory and nervous systems. See the light flowing into every dark corner. Use white light or a specific color, or simply allow the light to be the color determined by your subconscious mind.

7. If you know the specific body area that needs healing, gradually concentrate the light there and let it remain as long as required.

8. Gradually withdraw attention from the light as you affirm three times, aloud or silently, resting quietly a few moments between declarations: *God is life. I am one with God. I am one with life. Thank You, God, for perfect life. In the name and through the power of Jesus Christ, the Great Physician.* After the last declaration, say, *Amen.*

9. Rest quietly and without conscious

thought for at least a minute.

Of course, you may use affirmations of your own which have the same meanings as those given in the instructions. The words do not matter so long as they help you to release any unforgiving thoughts or feelings that may have blocked the free flow of the healing love and life of God.

Jesus advised us to forgive before we pray; so, by omitting step 7, the Fifteen-Minute Treatment can be used simply to clear the consciousness of unsuspected negative thoughts and feelings. It will still be a healing prayer technique, but one more concerned with the psyche or soul than with the body.

Balancing Masculine and Feminine Natures

Actually, to heal means more than to alleviate a physical ailment. It means also *to restore to original purity or integrity* and *to make a person whole.* Our bodies can be whole and functioning reasonably well while our psyches are out of kilter. Though any positive prayer technique helps to correct imbalance of the soul, there is one that has been specifically designed to help us balance the masculine and feminine sides of our nature.

Everyone has both natures, but in our culture boys are usually encouraged to develop their masculine side more than the feminine side, and girls are encouraged to develop their feminine side more than the masculine side. There is nothing wrong with the practice so long as it does not cripple the activity of the side that is subordinated, and so long as the individual feels free to express the subordinated nature whenever the expression is appropriate. Truly whole persons are those who have developed both sides equally, for both sides are important.

The masculine nature is the thinking, rational, action-oriented side which deals with the outer, public world, is competitive, controlling, and concerned with success and material life. The feminine nature is the feeling, intuitive, nurturing side which deals with personal relationships, is cooperative and supportive, and concerned with spiritual matters. Obviously, most women express some of their masculine side and most men express some of their feminine side; but we can all bring the two natures into better balance.

The prayer technique to balance the two natures requires that you pray the Lord's Prayer six or nine times a day for at least three weeks, a practice that is beneficial to spiritual well-being. It involves visualization, but unlike the techniques already given, it usually takes only about five minutes of your time two or three times a day.

Balancing Technique

(To be done morning, night, and midday if possible.)

1. Assume a comfortable, relaxed position, sitting or lying down.

2. In whatever way you wish, order your subconscious servant to have each side of your nature pray the Lord's Prayer by itself and then to have them pray the prayer together. Declare that you wish to have an image or symbol representing the highest development of each nature at the present moment when each prays alone and when the two pray together.

3. Let the first nature pray silently, and observe the image or impression you receive.

4. Let the second nature pray silently, and observe the image or impression you receive.

5. Let the two natures pray together

silently, and observe the image or impressions you receive.

6. Declare that God now reveals the meaning of what you have observed, and rest quietly a few moments.

The first images or impressions may or may not be human. Some persons receive images of animals, flowers, or other natural objects; some receive images of man-made things; some receive no visual impressions during the early sessions, but receive them later. Almost always the images change as the individuals understand their meanings. Those who persist with the exercise become better acquainted with themselves, learn what they need to do to develop aspects of themselves which they may have neglected, become more self-accepting and better able to express their whole selves.

This technique is equally effective when used by individuals who are not Christian and who prefer to use a great prayer of their own faith.

Regardless of the purpose of using visualization in prayer, its effectiveness probably results from our tendency to believe what we can see, whether with our physical eye or with the eyes of the mind. If we can mentally see ourselves or others enjoying good health or healing, prosperity, or harmonious relationships, or mentally see our masculine and feminine natures developing equally, we can believe or have faith in the desired outcome of our prayers.

So visualization is a way to pray in faith. In time, lengthy visualization work becomes unnecessary. The simple declaration *I see . . .* becomes sufficient to trigger the picture-making mechanism of imagination into forming a clear mental image of answered prayer for ourselves or others so that we are ready to do our part in claiming the good that God has prepared for all His children.

X

Guidance

Regardless of how or why we pray, the answers to prayers almost always involve guidance because, in one form or another, God has already supplied everything we need. But to have it, we must claim it, first in mind and then in the outer world. That means that after we realize that the good we seek is present, we usually must perform some outward acts to connect ourselves with it. Occasionally, all we must do is wait patiently and, while we go about our usual activities, simply know that the good is becoming manifest and remain alert to recognize it when it appears. More often, some time after we have prayed, we seem to know that we need to cooperate with God's activity by saying particular words and performing particular acts to assist in the manifestation process.

Standards for Guidance

Of course, we want to know how to be certain that guidance is from God, particularly if what we think is guidance coincides with what we thought we ought to do or what we wanted to do before we prayed. The first thing to remember is that we are children of God, so there is no reason to believe that what we think we ought to do or what we want to do is necessarily wrong. The second thing to remember is that the New Testament has supplied us with some standards to apply to guidance, whether it comes before or after prayer. The standards are clearly listed in The Letter of James. He writes: *But the wisdom from above is first pure, then peaceable, gentle, open to reason, full of mercy and good fruits, without uncertainty or insincerity.* (James 3:17)

The passage means that the guidance of God is free of selfish motives (pure), promotes harmony (peaceable), is considerate and courteous (gentle), allows for discussion, can be modified, and is ultimately logical (open to reason), is compassionate (full of mercy), and ultimately serves the best interest of everyone (good fruits), is impartial, straightforward, free of doubt, and honest (without uncertainty and insincerity). If any proposed course of action fulfills all those requirements (regardless of when or how you have conceived the course of action); you can follow it confidently, for it will be in accordance with God's will. If any attribute is missing, the wise person postpones action until he has received guidance with all the attributes of "wisdom from above."

Confirming Guidance

Although the standards listed in The Letter of James give us the best method for confirming guidance, we sometimes receive guidance which meets the standards but which we hesitate to follow; we may hesitate because the guidance requires us to say or do what seems too unusual, too daring, too uncomfortable, or even impossible for us. We may think, "God can't really mean that I am to do this!" At those times, we are much like Gideon, one of the judges of Israel. The Midianites had raided and harassed Israel for seven years, and God had indicated to Gideon that

he was the man to rid the land of the enemy.
When the Midianites and their allies massed
for attack in the Valley of Jezreel, Gideon
sounded the trumpet for the Israelites to
follow him. But after they gathered, Gideon
began to have doubts. He looked at the eager
but essentially untried troops with their
meager weapons, and he wondered if he had
understood his guidance correctly. Surely
God could not really mean that he should face
the well-seasoned enemy with such a raggle-
taggle crowd; it would be slaughtered immediately. So before Gideon went on with his
plans, this is what he did:

*Then Gideon said to God, "If thou wilt
deliver Israel by my hand, as thou has said,
behold, I am laying a fleece of wool on the
threshing floor; if there is dew on the fleece
alone, and it is dry on all the ground, then I
shall know that thou wilt deliver Israel by my
hand, as thou hast said." And it was so.
When he rose early next morning and
squeezed the fleece, he wrung enough dew
from the fleece to fill a bowl with water. Then
Gideon said to God, "Let not thy anger burn
against me, let me speak but this once; pray,
let me make trial only this once with the
fleece; pray, let it be dry only on the fleece,*

*and on all the ground let there be dew." And
God did so that night; for it was dry on the
fleece only, and on all the ground there was
dew.* (Judges 6:36-40)

Gideon was satisfied, and from then on,
even though much of the guidance seemed
strange, he did as God directed.

Gideon was not seeking guidance by his action and requests, he was asking for confirmation. We receive guidance either through
the thoughts that seem to come spontaneously when we are faced with some problem
or through the thoughts or urges that come
following prayer concerning some problem.
Either way, we are getting guidance from
God. If we think we may have misunder-
stood, we can do something that is rather like
what Gideon did. Of course, we do not ask
God to do strange tricks. We can use any of
four simple methods.

Almost always, the first outward step required to follow guidance is rather easily
accomplished. Gideon had no trouble gather-
ing an army. In fact, when you read the rest
of the story, you will see that when Gideon
finally decided to continue following his ini-
tial guidance, God told him to reduce his
troops until he had only 300 men! Far more

men had answered Gideon's call to arms than God needed to do the work.

Gideon had already received confirmation of the guidance because the first step was relatively easy to accomplish.

A second method to confirm guidance is to check how you feel. Most of us experience certain feelings that tell us that what we are doing is right. For one person, the feeling might be a sense of joy; for another it might be a warm sensation in the solar plexus; for another it might be an urge to sing a song or to whistle. Remember how or what you felt when you did what you were convinced God had guided you to do and everything turned out right for you and everyone else. If that feeling is present, the guidance is confirmed.

The third method is a bit more complicated. At some time when you are not faced with the necessity to confirm guidance, ask in prayer to be given two signals—one that will always mean "yes" and one that will always mean "no."

A Confirmation Technique

Here is a way to receive your own signals:
1. Assume a comfortable, relaxed posi-

tion, sitting or lying down.

2. Affirm silently or aloud: *I am in the presence of God, and God is present in me.* Repeat the affirmation several times until you feel the truth of it. Then repeat three times: *My mind is one with the Mind of God.*

3. Declare silently or aloud the following statements or some of your own with the same meanings: *Father, I desire to do only Your will. When I am uncertain that I have understood it, I desire to be told if I am right or if I am wrong. I now accept a sign for yes and a sign for no.*

4. Rest quietly, and silently think the word *yes* several times, pausing each time and waiting for a signal.

The signal may come immediately, it may come after several sessions of asking, or it may not seem to come. If you already have a reliable means of confirming guidance, your subconscious mind may not give you a new sign. Most signs are very ordinary sensations which we associate with being correct—a feeling of relief or joy, the sight of green for "go ahead," perhaps the word "yes" seeming to sound in our minds; but sometimes someone receives a signal that is startling or even ridiculous. If that happens, it is probably because only that kind of sign will get the person's attention.

5. After you receive the sign for *yes,* silently think the word *no* several times, pausing each time and waiting for a signal.

Both signals are important. Even if you have not asked for guidance, your sign for *no* often occurs spontaneously if you start to do something not in your best interests or in the best interests of someone else. A man who received a sneeze for *yes* received the word *stop* for *no.* He sometimes hears "stop" in his head when he should discontinue some action; more frequently, he becomes aware that someone or something stops him. He does not simply try to find a way to do what he has set out to do; he stops and prays for guidance.

6. Whether or not you think you have received signals, close the prayer session with thanksgiving.

Almost always, the signals are simple, definite, and unmistakable. They arise from within your own being and are impressed on your own subconscious mind which can be trusted to bring them to your awareness when you need them. A personal example may clarify what I mean. My own signals are very ordinary—green for *yes,* and red for *no.* One time when puzzled by guidance about a situation in the church to which I ministered, in my morning prayers at home I asked to be given clear and definite indication that I either had or had not understood correctly. Not until I arrived at the door of the church in record time did I realize that my guidance had been confirmed. My home was twenty-two miles from the church. During the entire drive, I had had to stop only at the boulevard stop sign near my home. All traffic lights—even those for left turns—had been green when I had reached them. I am not suggesting that God had gone before me and adjusted the traffic lights for my benefit. I believe that my subconscious mind caused me to adjust my driving speed so that it coordinated with the regular timing of the traffic lights. After all, I was driving a habitual route, and though I was not consciously aware of the intervals between traffic signals, the intervals were impressed on my subconscious mind. The "green light" was given to the puzzling course of action. I took the first step, and the rest was easy.

A fourth way to confirm guidance is to decide for yourself what is to be the signal for *yes* in a specific situation about which you have prayed. The signal should be some action or event that is unusual but not impossible, and it should bear a relationship to the challenge about which you have received the guidance. Once again, an example will clarify what I mean.

A well-qualified woman who worked for a charitable organization had for six months temporarily filled an executive position which traditionally was filled by a noted man. Her work was excellent. One day she was told that her appointment would probably be permanent. But the next day, just before closing time, the personnel committee met with her to tell her that another well-known man had expressed interest in the position. They were considering engaging him and returning her to her former duties. Trying to hide her shock and dismay, she said that she would do what was best for the organization. When she got home, she spent an hour or so dealing with her anger. After she had become calm, she wrote a letter to God which declared that He was in charge of the organization and that He would guide her to do what was best for her and the organization. She felt a sense of release and slept well. Next morning, after prayers, these words came into her mind, "If you were a man with your qualifications and record, the committee would not consider replacing you; and if you were a man, you would not have said what you said." She had to agree. Then she asked, "What should I do?" The answer came, "Call the committee together and tell what you have heard."

The guidance was anything but comfortable. In the first place, the committee was composed of unpaid volunteers who were successful, busy men. In the second place, calling the committee together was not one of her privileges. In the third place, acting outside her privileges was totally out of character for her. She felt frightened, but she knew that she had to act at once on the guidance before the committee had time to speak to the man. She also knew that if she was supposed to call the committee together, the way would be easy. For her, the easy way would be to have one member of the committee contact her early, and that is what she declared would happen if her guidance was correct. It was a very unusual event for which she asked; but it happened.

Soon after she arrived at work, the chairman came to her office to request information about a worker in her department who was being considered for promotion. She gave the information and then said, "I would appreciate meeting with the committee before it meets with Mr. _____." The chairman said that a meeting would be possible in an hour. At the meeting, she said, "If I were a man with my qualifications and record, you would not consider replacing me with another man; but if you did, I would not meekly agree to go back to my old job." There was a brief silence during which the members looked at one another. Then first one and then all the others nodded. The chairman said, "You are right." She retained her position for many years. The man they had thought of hiring was given a similar position in another organization.

When she told me of her experience, she said, "I believe that had I not received the guidance and then asked for that particular confirmation signal, I would probably have reacted negatively to the early morning visit from the chairman. I would have thought he was being inconsiderate to ask for my help after telling me that I was probably going to be demoted. As it was, I saw the visit positively, as an opportunity not an insult, so I was able to do what I needed to do."

Persons who regularly practice positive prayer become so conscious of the abiding presence of God that they rarely need to confirm guidance. Their minds are always open to it, and they feel increasingly secure enough and willing to do as God directs. Nevertheless, when faced with a situation in which the best course of action seems too unusual, daring, uncomfortable, or even impossible for them, they usually ask for some kind of confirmation; when it comes, they confidently follow the guidance. They ... *know that in everything God works for good with those who love him, who are called according to his purpose.* (Rom. 8:28)

XI

Nine-Hour Prayer Vigil Or Novena

Often we are faced with situations or circumstances about which we can do nothing but pray and have faith in God's will for the good of all His children. At such times, practitioners of positive prayer can avoid heaping up *"empty phrases"* (Matt. 6:7) by conducting a nine-hour prayer vigil, an adaptation of the novena.

In the Roman Catholic church, a novena is a nine-day devotion for a religious intention. Every day for nine days, a person prays a specific prayer for a specific reason. Usually, well before the novena is completed, the petitioner receives a sense of peace about the intention but continues to pray until the novena is completed. In the ancient symbolism of numbers, nine represents completion, attainment, fulfillment, the end of a cycle of activity; so we can understand why the practice of praying nine times was established.

A novena provides a way to be persistent in prayer. Jesus illustrated the efficacy of persistent prayer with the parable of the widow and the unrighteous judge. She went many times to ask him for help, and he kept turning her away until her persistence wore him down, and he granted her request. Jesus concluded the parable by saying that if an unrighteous judge could be persuaded by persistent petition to treat someone justly, certainly God would not delay. (Luke 18:1-8)

Jesus also advocated persistency in prayer when He said: *"Ask, and it will be given you; seek, and you will find; knock, and it will be opened to you."* (Matt. 7:7) The word *knock* suggests repetition. The word *open* implies the removal of a barrier. Repeated prayer removes any mental barrier between us and our recognition of the good we seek or between our consciousness and the guidance we need to assist in the manifestation of our good.

Catholic friends who introduced me to the practice many years ago reported such satisfactory results after conducting novenas that I adapted the custom to the positive prayer mode. In times of urgent need, I have found that compressing the novena to nine hours has been particularly effective. I have used it for my own needs or for the needs of others. I have taught it to prayer groups and classes to use for prayer chain work in emergencies.

When you use the nine-hour prayer vigil for someone else, try to have the other person keep the vigil, too. But even if the other person cannot keep the vigil, or if he or she is unaware of what you are doing, the vigil will be effective.

The Process

The simple process is as follows:

1. Once every hour (preferably at the same time) for nine hours in a row (even if that means setting an alarm clock to awaken you during the night), say the following prayer or a similar one:

Jesus said: *"Ask, and it will be given you; seek, and you will find; knock, and it will be opened to you."*

Father, I ask, I seek, I knock. And I know that You are at work to bring about (here you insert a phrase that summarizes the purpose of the prayer; i.e. perfect healing, right solutions, divine order, justice, peace and harmony, abundant supply, etc.).

2. Affirm the presence of whatever specific good you are seeking. Here are some examples of what you might say: *I see Mary whole and free; her leg is healed, and she can walk. I now find the perfect job at the perfect pay where I can serve in a perfect way. My relationship with my brother is peaceful and harmonious.*

3. Conclude the prayer session with a statement like this: *I thank You, Father, that You hear me always and provide for every need.*

4. If, as often happens when one is conducting a nine-hour prayer vigil, you receive a sense of peace before the ninth hour, continue to pray each hour but stress your gratitude for peace of mind in steps 1 and 2 by using words like these: *I am grateful for peace of mind as I pray.*

5. After the ninth prayer session say: *I place* (insert whatever the specific concern has been: i.e. Mary's healing, my employment, the relationship with my brother) *lovingly in Your hands, Father.* You may,

of course, rephrase this prayer to suit your-self.

6. After the nine-hour prayer vigil is over, if concern about the matter reasserts itself, gently dismiss the thought with a declaration like this: *I have placed _____ lovingly in the hands of God. God is in charge, and all is well.*

Sometimes, after the third or fourth prayer session of a nine-hour vigil, you may forget to pray at the appointed time. Do not feel guilty or flustered. Your forgetfulness is a sign that the sense of urgency has lessened and you have begun to release the matter into God's hands. Simply resume the process as soon as you remember, and stress your gratitude.

Of course, you can conduct a nine-day or a nine-week prayer vigil if you wish. Longer periods may be required to release concern over the matter about which you are praying. For instance, a nine-week prayer vigil might help you to have peace of mind about a par-ticular world, national, civic, or organiza-tional situation and help you to take con-structive action.

Regardless of the reason for conducting a prayer vigil, the vigil increases the amount of time spent in conscious communion with God and strengthens one's sense of the presence of God.

XII

By the Grace of God

The more we pray, the more we experience the grace of God, until we finally realize that we live by grace.

Grace is God's gift of love and mercy, given freely to us whether or not we deserve it. We cannot steal, borrow, buy, or earn it. We can only accept or refuse it.

We accept and experience grace whenever we realize that we have not had to pay the price for some negative thought, word, or action, or when we recognize that in some mysterious way we have been protected in adverse or dangerous circumstances. Everyone has had such experiences, and anyone can become ready to be conscious of the ever-present grace of God by practicing positive prayer.

Positive prayer readies us to recognize and accept grace because it is a process of repentance. Theologians agree that repentance readies one to accept grace. *To repent* means more than to be sorry and make amends for erroneous thoughts, words, and deeds—though certainly this is an important meaning; *to repent* also means to change one's thoughts. Actually, only by changing our thoughts can we be sorry and make amends for what we have thought, said, and done.

By helping us to eliminate negative and to acquire positive thoughts about our relationship with God, our fellow human beings, and the universe, and about our own nature and potential for good, positive prayer prepares us to accept the ever-present activity of the love and mercy of God in our lives.

Grace is not a special activity of God reserved only for human emergencies. It is omnipresent. As the principle which governs the cosmic process and as the cosmic process itself, God is always pouring out love and mercy. We *"live and move and have our being..."* (Acts 17:28) in God, in the cosmic process; and the cosmic process is always working to produce the highest and best conditions for all its products.

Positive prayer aligns our minds with the flow of the cosmic process so that we consciously think, speak, and act in harmony with it—we live in harmony with it. To live in harmony with the flow of the cosmic process is analogous to driving toward a desired destination on a great road or freeway system, obeying the signals and road signs and honoring the speed limits. We will travel safely and arrive at our destination at the right time. We know the possible consequences of a driver's ignorantly, carelessly, or willfully running a red light, going the wrong way on a one-way street, or entering a freeway on an exit ramp. In much the same way, most tribulations result from attempts to oppose the flow of the cosmic process. But we know that many times when we have been headed for danger, something has mysteriously intervened to turn us away or around toward safety. That "something" is grace, and the fact that we have not had to deal with the consequences of all our transgressions of cosmic or divine law is ample evidence of the omnipresence of grace.

As you regularly practice positive prayer, you will realize that whether or not you have known it, you have always been helped by the grace of God. As you keep your thoughts, feelings, beliefs, and attitudes in harmony with the flow of the cosmic process, you will know that Paul was speaking to you when he said: *And my God will supply every need of yours according to his riches in glory in Christ Jesus. To our God and Father be glory for ever and ever. Amen.* (Phil. 4:19, 20)

Printed U.S.A.

56-1676-8M-9-89